CELEBRITY JUICE

THE BOOK

This edition first published in Great Britain in 2013
by Orion Books
an imprint of the Orion Publishing Group Ltd
Orion House, 5 Upper St Martin's Lane,
London WC2H 9EA
An Hachette UK Company

1 3 5 7 9 10 8 6 4 2

A CIP catalogue record for this book is available
from the British Library.

ISBN (hardback): 9781 4091 2756 7
ISBN (trade paperback): 9781 4091 12757 4

Printed in Germany

People Who Helped Make This Book: Les Keen,
Ed Sleeman, Leon Wilson, Helen Zaltzman
Editorial: Helen Zaltzman, Jane Sturrock
and Nicola Crossley
Art Direction: Helen Ewing
Design: Goldust Design

The Orion Publishing Group's policy is to use papers
that are natural, renewable and recyclable and
made from wood grown in sustainable forests. The
logging and manufacturing processes are expected
to conform to the environmental regulations of the
country of origin.

PICTURE CREDITS
Getty: page 6, 17 (top right/ top left), 36 (top), 47
(top right), 51 (top middle/ top, far left/ top, far
right/ bottom, far right/ middle, far left), 61 (bottom
left),70, 75 (top right/ top left/ bottom right/ middle
right) 82, 83, 94 (left), 104 (top left), 105 (bottom),
106 (top), 108, 110, 111 (all, except for middle right
and top far right), 129 (top left/ middle left/ top
middle/ top right), 133; NL-HaNA, ANEFO / neg.
stroken, 1945-1989, 2.24.01.05, item number <922-
2262>: CC-BY-SA: page 129 (bottom right); Rex
Features: 17 (bottom), 42 (bottom far left/ bottom
middle left), 45 (top left/ top right/ middle left/
bottom right/ bottom left), 46 (middle left/ bottom
right/ top right), 47 (bottom right); Seth Poppel/
Yearbook Library: 44 (top right), 45 (top middle),
47 (top left); Shutterstock.com: page 5 (bottom
right), 23 (bottom), 28, 29 (bottom/ centre), 30, 31,
40, 43 (bottom far right), 43 (bottom far left/ bottom
middle right), 51 (middle right/ bottom middle/
bottom left), 55 (bottom right), 61, 69, 71, 82, 88,
94 (middle/ right), 95, 105 (top), 106 (bottom), 107,
108 (Joan Collins), 111 (top far right/ bottom far
right), 113, 121, 127, 129 (centre/ middle right), 130,
131, 135, 140, 142 (top left), 141, 142, 143, 144,
145 (flags), 152; Featureflash/ Shutterstock.com:
page 55 (bottom right), 129 (middle right); s_bukley/
Shutterstock.com: page 51 (bottom left); TalkBack:
page 4 (left/ middle), 5 (middle), 7, 11, 12, 13, 18,
19, 23 (top/ middle), 25, 26 (top), 27, 28/29 (centre),
33, 34, 35, 39, 42, 43, 46 (bottom left), 52 (top), 53
(top right/top/ top left), 54 (top/ bottom), 55 (top
right/ bottom left), 56, 57, 58, 59, 60, 61 (middle/
top), 63, 64, 65, 66, 67, 68, 72, 73, 78, 82, 84, 85,
96, 100, 101, 102, 103, 115, 116, 117, 118, 119, 120
(top), 123, 124, 125, 126, 136, 137, 138, 139, 146,
148, 149, 153, 154, 155; TalkBack/Rex Features:
page 46 (middle right), 47 (bottom left) WENN:
page 44 (top left), 46 (top middle).

Every effort has been made to fulfil requirements
with regard to reproducing copyright material.
The author and publisher will be glad to rectify
any omissions at the earliest opportunity.

www.orionbooks.co.uk

My name is

....
write your name, you dingbat

I am .... years old

I live in a palace/moonbase/
submarine/caravan/skip
delete as applicable

In my imagination, I am

....

But in reality I am

....

This book belongs to me.

Contents

PART 1

PART 2

PART 3

Dear Readers

Congratulations! You are currently holding in your hands the total combined knowledge of everything that we, the producers of Celebrity Juice, have learnt making the show since 2008. Plus lots and lots of new things we made up just for this book.

WHAT YOU WILL FIND IN THIS BOOK:

1) Stuff about Celebrity Juice. Duh.

2) Everything* you need to know to play Celebrity Juice with your friends and family in the comfort of your own home, school or institution.

3) All your favourite characters from the show, including The Keith Lemon Information Technology Supercomputer, Gary (RIP) and Spud The Dog, and not forgetting the most Bangra Tidy man on the planet, Indian Keith.

The book brings together all of your favourite games from the show to play with your mates, so join your favourite team and play Celebrity Juice with Keith, Holly and Fearne and get involved in three hilarious parts – from Keith's Scotch Egg Club and The Moob to Be A Dingbat and Touch the Cardboard. In between parts, test your knowledge of the show with the Celebrity Juice quizzes, puzzle over the Suboku and relive the top 10 funniest moments on the show.

Now all you need to do is pick your teams – we suggest the sexiest man in the house being Keith, the woman with the biggest bangers being Holly and the youngest boy in the house being F...reddie the show's accountant. Finally the prettiest girl should be Fearne (hey, what did you think we were going to say?).

So get your mates over, pour a few pints of Celebrity Juice, give yourselves an allotted time and have a truckload of fun.

Lots of love,

The Producers of Celebrity Juice

* Except a TV studio, sets, expensive cameras, a 400-strong live audience and celebrity panellists – but trust us, all those things are overrated.

TOP 3
FAVOURITE
MOMENTS OF

CELEBRITY JUICE

3. JEDWARD'S ATTACK DOG CHALLENGE

We sent a police attack dog after Jedward and Keith. The winner was whoever managed to run the furthest before being caught by the canine cop. Keith emerged victorious; Jedward emerged lightly nibbled.

2. TICKLE MONSTER

The moment when Holly gets wrestled to the floor by the Tickle Monster. Tickle-phobic Holly discovered her worst nightmare when she came face to face with The Tickle Monster. In fact, she nearly pissed herself! I tickle your mum!

1. KEITH CHASING VERNE

Keith and Verne Troyer re-enact Jurassic Park through the power of mime. If you haven't seen it yet then what the hell are you doing reading this book? Get on YouTube now and find it!

Producers' Notes

ROUNDS BRAINSTORM

NB — Tom insists on ndnrg bareback

CRUISIN FOR A BRUISIN
Guests take on Tom Cruise in a boxing match dangling from the ceiling on wires.

KEITH VERSUS SHARK *rehersal left four cameramen dead*

HANK ME OFF
Tom Hanks rides the guests around a showjumping course set up in the studio. They win points if they can buck him.

SWASH STICKER *— like the game but can we think of another title?*
Joe Swash is covered in glue and has thirty seconds in which to stick as many things to himself as he can.

BEERNARDO DiCAPRIO
Leonardo DiCaprio challenges guests to a drinking competition. *prior filming commitments with Scorsese*

NEIL OR NO NEIL
Like Deal or No Deal except instead of money, the contestant has to guess which red box Neil Buchanan is hiding in. *check whether Neil Buchanan is too tall to fit in a box*

DISCO IN FEARNE-NOSE
Hold a disco in Fearne's nostrils. *could prove fatal if Fearne has a cold that day*

FRIDGE FAZER
How long can Fazer survive in a fridge freezer?

HARRY'S TILES *BORING!!!*
Harry Styles retiles a bathroom in real time. Panels have to guess how long it'll take him.

KATIE PRICE IS RIGHT
Contestants have to try to win an argument against Katie Price. *IMPOSSIBLE*

GLASS HOFF FULL
Contestants have to guess how many jellybeans there are in a Hoff-shaped jamjar. *??*
The closest guess wins the jellybeans.

?? will insurance cover this?

HEX FACTOR

The contestant who can cast the most damaging curse wins a point.

T-REX FACTOR

Each team member mentors a dinosaur to become an amazing singer, voting out one each episode. *Props dept can't source enough dinosaurs.*
Keep on ice until Jurassic Park becomes a reality.

CHEQUES FACTOR

Each panellist has to give a cheque to us producers. The one who gives us the most money wins! *nobody uses cheques any more, consider updating to PayPal*

POLITE CLUB

Like Fight Club except instead of punching each other, contestants have to pay each other compliments. The nicest player wins a point for their team.
Completely wrong for Juice. Pitch to BBC4

AMERICAN FRUITY

Teams have to guess the mystery celebrity posing seductively under a pile of fruit.

HOLLYOATS

Holly Willoughbooby has to eat as much porridge as possible in 30 seconds. ✓

HAVE I GOT GLUES FOR YOU *NB very painful for hairy celebs*

Each guest is doused in glue and stuck to the studio wall. The one who is last to fall off wins a point.

SALAD SNOOKER

Teams have to pot 15 tomatoes, an onion, an apple, a potato, a mouldy potato, a beetroot and a really really mouldy potato, using a boiled egg as the cueball and a stick of celery as the cue. *needs vinaigrette?*

WEST ON SUPER MARE *— room in the budget for this as well as Keith's hairdresser?*

Buy a really good mare and make Kanye West compete on it in the Grand National.

McFLYING WITHOUT WINGS

Fire McFly out of a canon. The one who goes furthest wins a point.
Health and safety gone MAD

CELEBRITY JUICE   10 BUMMINGTON PLACE, MOTTSVILLE

9

Introducing...

Keith

FACT FILE

Full name: Keith Ian Lemon
Nick name: Don't have one
Date of birth: None of your bee's wax
Born and raised: Leeds
Height: Taller than Michael J Fox, around 6 foot-ish
Education: Yes, educated in life
Family: Yeah I got a mum and a bruv, who is gay. Not me mum, me bruv
Hair colour: Strawberry blond
Star sign: I'm not really into that stuff. I'd like a star on me dressing room door though
First job: Leeds market

If you could have any superpower, what would it be and why? Read me book, *Being Keith*, it's in there. I love the idea of having a super power and using it for good!

If you could choose an alternate career, what would you choose and why? I'd be a singer/rapper, cos I've been told I'm very good at it.

What do you think you would be doing if you weren't on Celebrity Juice? *Through The Key Hole* and *Lemon La Vida Loca* I guess. I'd like to do a period drama though.

Who would be your dream date and why? At the moment I'm dating Jenny Powell an' I really like her. I'd love to have a go on Natalie Imbruglia though.

Who has been your favourite celebrity guest? Pissed up Gareth Gates.

Who has been your least favourite celebrity guest and why? Anyone I've never heard of. I'd name names but I can't remember their names.

If you could go on holiday with anybody on the show, who would it be and why? Holly and Fearne, to Amsterdam.

What is your favourite Celebrity Juice game? Shouting One Out or Touch The Cardboard.

If you could be stranded on a desert island with three objects, what would you take and why? Me iPad, so I could Skype me mates and do emails and such, a knife for killing wild boars and a flame thrower for self defense and making fires.

Fearne

If you could have any superpower, what would it be and why? To be able to run really quickly like the vampires in *Twilight*. I have dreams I can do that.

If you could choose an alternate career, what would you choose and why? Definitely a cake maker. I would have a little cafe and sell beautiful cakes. There's still time...

What do you think you would be doing if you weren't on Celebrity Juice? Baking cakes/eating cakes/sniffing cakes! Working on my Radio 1 show and my clothing range, doing loads of charity stuff and hanging with my boy, Rex.

Who would be your dream date and why? Dave Grohl. He's funny, lovely, clever and hairy.

Who has been your favourite celebrity guest and why? I loved Verne Troyer and Jason Biggs from *American Pie*.

Who has been your least favourite celebrity guest, and why? All of our guests have been entertaining. I was terrified of Janice Dickinson at first but I ended up really liking her!

If you could go on holiday with anybody on the show, who would it be and why? Holly! We've had some fun times over the years, one being a holiday to LA when we were about 24. We laughed a lot!

What is your favourite Celebrity Juice game? Shouting One Out is always ridiculously mad. And Who Are You Kidding because I'm pretty good at it. It's a useless skill to have in life but I've got it.

If you could be stranded on a desert island with three objects, what would you take and why? A Kitchenaid so I could make cakes, an iPod to listen to music and a bed. Practical I love sleep too much.

Holly

FACT FILE

Full name: Holly Willoughby
Nick name: Willoughhooby
Date of birth: 10th February 1981
Born and raised: Brighton
Height: 5 foot 7 inches
Education: School
Family: Yes
Hair colour: Blonde
Star sign: Aquarius
First job: Garden centre checkout girl

If you could have any superpower, what would it be and why? I would love the power of invisibility. The first thing I would do is go to Buckingham Palace and see what the Queen is up to.

If you could choose an alternate career, what would you choose and why? I always said that I would like to own a cattery, I hope that doesn't make me sound like a weird cat lady, I'm thinking more of a cat hotel...

What do you think you would be doing if you weren't on Celebrity Juice? I love the show and if I wasn't working I would definitely be sat at home watching it!

Who would be your dream date and why? I have a top three and I'm not sure which order they would go in. I've always had soft spots for Michael Bublé, Rupert Penry Jones and Robert Pattison.

Who has been your favourite celebrity guest and why? I love when Phil's on because it's when people get to see the real him and how naughty he can be.

Who has been your least favourite celebrity guest, and why? Most people know what to expect and even people whom you have a pre-conceived idea about, you get to see a different side, which is fun!

If you could go on holiday with anybody on the show, who would it be and why? Definitely not Keith. Probably Kelly or Indian Keith because I feel I hardly know him.

What is your favourite Celebrity Juice game? I love the Mask of Sorrow. It's so ridiculous and Keith can say those things that everyone is thinking but wouldn't dare say.

If you could be stranded on a desert island with three objects, what would you take and why? My phone so I could contact the outside word and call for help to get me off the island, some factor 30 so I don't end up looking like Keith, and a bottle of tequila.

PLAY AT HOME
MENU

APPETISERS £2.99

Furry cup-a-soup

Chris Tarrantasalata with Brad Pitta

Flan B √

ChoriZoe Ball

Quiche Duffy

Carol Vol-au-vents

FISH £6.99

Mel C-food salad

Professor Bream

Hake That

Geri Hallibut

Salmon Mark

Prawn Ryder

Squid Vicious

Clamela Anderson

ITALIAN £6.99

Alan Carrbonara

Pizza Andre √

Jizzotto

Rigatoni Cotton

Penne Lancaster √

David SpaGuetta √

Nancy Dell'Olio

CLASSICS £7.99

Justin Bieburger

Will.i.ham egg and chips

Russell Brandwich √

Katy Peri Peri

Dane Bowers's toe in your hole

Bangers and mash your back doors in

Richard Hammond cheese toastie √

Louis Walsh rarebit √

Rod Stewpot

Mickey Pork

PAN-ASIAN STATION £5.99

Tiny Tempura √

Seth Rogan josh

Sophie Dahl

Katie Rice √

Bruno Mars-ala

John Teriyaki

Holly Willoughbeef in black bean sauce

SIDE DISHES £1.00

Premiership spit-roast Potatoes √

Cee-Lo Greens √

Davina McCauliflower √

Cheryl Coleslaw √

Bread Sheeran √

PiccaLily Allen √

Miranda Hartichokes √

Angelina Joleeks

DESSERT £3.99

Keith Lemon drizzle cake

Keith Lemon meringue pie

TiramiSuBo

Cake Winslet

Kate Mousse

The Saturdays' selection of tarts

Fearne Cotton candy

Emma Bunton

Hugh Lauriepops

Jodie Marshmallows

Jelly Osbourne

BEVERAGES £2.25

Britney Beers on tap   David Tennant's Super
Penis Grigio   Lemonade
Gary Barlow-water

PLAY CELEBRITY JUICE AT HOME

You don't need a professional TV production crew to play in the comfort of your own home. You just need this book and some friends to play with. For extra juiciness, you can construct your own Celebrity Juice studio using ordinary household objects. Go on, we'll wait.

DIFFICULTY RATING:

★★★★★★★★★★★ Impossible
★★★★★★★★★★ Very hard
★★★★★★★★★ Very hard
★★★★★★★★ Very hard
★★★★★★★ Very hard
★★★★★★ Moderate
★★★★★ Moderate
★★★★ Moderate
★★★ Moderate
★★ Simple as peas
★ For dingbats

OK, are you ready for some Celebrity Juice games?

 Yes Yes, as soon as I've finished my cup of tea

Turn the page and keep turning until you find a game you want to play.

BE A DINGBAT ✷

Generally in life it's best not to be a dingbat, but in this game you'll actually be rewarded if you *are* a dingbat.

PART 1

INSTRUCTIONS:

Turn off the lights. The questioner and the questionee sit opposite each other in the dark using torches to light their faces. Other players should take the opportunity to have a kip, scratch their bum or rearrange their tackle during the blackout.

The questioner poses rapid-fire questions to the questionee and the questionee wins a point if they are a dingbat and answer incorrectly, which is actually the correct thing to do. So if you're right, you're wrong, and if you're wrong, you're right – which presumably means you're actually wrong – which we guess means you're then right – which we suppose causes you to be wrong. Anyway, it's confusing. Just remember: be a dingbat.

If a contestant hesitates in giving an answer, they fail to score a point on account of being a dingbat – which should mean they score a point, but in this case doesn't. As we say, it's confusing.

FOR EXAMPLE:

Q. **What colour is an orange?**
A. **Any colour other than orange**

Q. **Tom Cruise is well known for being a famous what?**
A. **Any job other than actor**

Q. **What is the opposite of up?**
A. **Up**

Q. **What type of animal is Shaun the Sheep?**
A. **Any animal other than a sheep**

Q. **Fearne Cotton is known for having big what?**
A. **Any body part other than nostrils**

As well as not being a real dingbat, here are some other things that Stacey is not:

Stacey   Roland Rat

Rastamouse   Splinter from *Teenage Mutant Ninja Turtles*

JUICY TIPS

An expert 'Be a Dingbat' player won't just get the answers wrong, they'll do it in an amusing way that makes people laugh. Otherwise the round will probably be cut in the edit.

One of the most successful players of the game is sexy rodent-alike Stacey Solomon. Study Stacey's answers to learn how a true professional plays the game.

Q. What is the name of this show?
A. *The X Factor*

Q. What is the colour of Keith's hair?
A. Grey

Q. What disease did Cheryl Cole get last year?
A. Chlamydia

Q. Jeremy Clarkson is not a what?
A. Bumhole

Q. How many legs does Heather Mills have?
A. 5

Q. Who are these two? (above)
A. Ant and Dec

Q. Complete the name of this dating show – '*Take Me....*'?
A. To Bed

Stacey truly proved herself to 'Be a Dingbat' thus proving that she is not actually a dingbat. We think.

SCOTCH EGG CLUB

WARNING!
Dangers of
Scotch Egg Club:

1. Increased cholesterol due to dangerous levels of Scotch egg consumption.
2. Ongoing war with Pork Pie Club.

1. FIRST RULE OF SCOTCH EGG CLUB:
YOU DO NOT TALK ABOUT SCOTCH EGG CLUB.

2. SECOND RULE OF SCOTCH EGG CLUB:
YOU DO NOT TALK ABOUT SCOTCH EGG CLUB.

3. THIRD RULE OF SCOTCH EGG CLUB:
IF IT'S YOUR FIRST NIGHT AT SCOTCH EGG
CLUB YOU MUST EAT A SCOTCH EGG.

Before you turn the page, you must locate and eat a Scotch egg.
Are you done? Yes [ ] No [ ]
OK. YOU'RE IN.

WELCOME TO SCOTCH EGG CLUB
- - - - - - - - - - -

UPON SUPPLYING A PICTURE OF YOU WITH FIVE SCOTCH EGGS IN YOUR MOUTH YOU WILL RECEIVE YOUR OFFICIAL MEMBERSHIP CARD, SCOTCH EGG CLUB TIE, AND HOURLY NEWSLETTER.

If you break any of the rules of Scotch Egg Club, you will be killed by one of the following methods:

- Being pummelled in the arse by stale Scotch eggs
- Being thrown under a gigantic rolling Scotch egg
- Being stuffed full of Scotch eggs till you vom all over yourself
- Being covered in sausage meat, rolled in breadcrumbs, thrown into a vat of boiling oil and cooked until you are a human Scotch egg

SPOT THE SCOTCH EGGS! ✸ ✸

There are 10 mini Scotch eggs hidden below. Can you spot them all?

SCOTCH EGG CHALLENGE ★★★★★

NUMBER OF PLAYERS: 3

EQUIPMENT:

1 giant Scotch egg

Lots of mini Scotch eggs

INSTRUCTIONS:

Elect one player to be the Scotch Egg Master. The other two players are pitted against each other.

The Scotch Egg Master hides behind the doors in the giant Scotch egg. (If your giant Scotch egg doesn't have doors, you can buy some from Ikea. If you don't have a giant Scotch egg, the Scotch Egg Master can hide in the bath behind the shower curtain and whip it open when ready.)

The Scotch Egg Master poses with a mini Scotch egg. When the doors fly open, the first player to spot the mini Scotch egg wins.

Repeat until all the mini Scotch eggs have gone rancid.

SHOUTING ONE OUT ★★★★★★★★

This game is the opposite of Chinese whispers, hence the original name 'Chinese shouting'.

PLAYERS: 3 contestants, 1 toilet attendant

SMELLINESS: 4

EQUIPMENT:

Public toilet

3 MP3 players with noise-cancelling headphones

3 pairs of skivvies

INSTRUCTIONS:

Find a public toilet with holes in the cubicle walls at ear-height. Maybe give the walls a quick clean with an antiseptic wipe.

The three contestants sit on the toilet in three adjacent cubicles.

The contestants drop their skivvies around their ankles and put the headphones on, turning the music up to full blast.

The elected toilet attendant selects a piece of graffiti off the toilet wall, and shouts it through the hole in the wall to the first contestant.

The contestant repeats the message to the next contestant, who repeats it to the third.

The last contestant shouts out what they think they heard.

If you don't have a public toilet, you can use your toilet at home: seat the three contestants on chairs next to each other, use a washable marker pen to daub the tiles with graffiti, then play as above.

For a good time call

58008

TOILET-THEMED SONGS

'Float On' by Modest Mouse

'Push It' by Salt-N-Pepa

'The Urinal Countdown' by Europe'

'Boom Boom Poo' by Black Eyed Poos

'Crapper's Delight' by The Sugarhill Gang

DON'T HASSLE THE HOFF WHEN HE'S WEEING

✗ YOUR MUM

NO SHITER
NO LIKEY ☺

FUN FACT
No one has ever won
a single point playing
this game on
Celebrity Juice

GOLDEN
POTATO

FOR A
Mediocre
Time
CaLL
5537 8008

Here are some examples of what people actually said when playing Shouting One Out on Celebrity Juice:

1

What Keith said: Deirdre came in here without her glasses on the other week, I hardly recognised her.

What Holly heard: Deirdre came in here the other week without her cl*t***s on, I hardly recognised her.

What Jack P. Shepherd heard: Deirdre walks in my house the other night and asks for a small dinosaur.

**What it ended up being:
Jack Sparrow has got smallpox.**

2

What Keith said: When I took my car into the arches, I saw Phil Mitchell waxing his bald head.

What Fearne heard: I saw my cat in a garage, and he had a bald head.

What it ended up being: I saw my dad licking my granny, she was a boiled egg.

3

What Keith said: Caroline and Harry are getting back together, she loves his baby face.

What Holly heard: Caroline and Harry are getting back together, she loves his p***s.

What it ended up being: Brethren, brethren, we've been together!

4

What Keith said: Cheryl Cole got a bit punchy in here the other day, must be her time of the month.

What Fearne heard: Cheryl Cole got a bit pushy the other day because it's her time of the month.

What it ended up being: Cheryl Cole has got a bit podgy... I think Matt's f****d your mum.

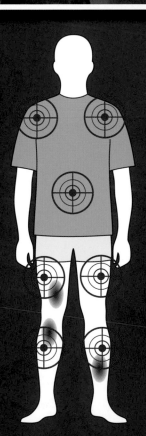

> Go on, bring it … just do it.

> Y'alright Danny?

> Yeah...

THE BAGUETTE-BEATER CHALLENGE ★★

PLAYERS: 2

PAIN LEVEL: ★★★★

EQUIPMENT:

Baguettes

Optional: stereotypical French outfit of beret, stripy top and onion necklace

INSTRUCTIONS:

Each player is armed with a baguette.

Players take it in turns to hit their opponent with the baguette.

The person whose baguette breaks into the most pieces is the winner.

LEVLELS:

EASY: Fresh baguette
MODERATE: Stale baguette
ADVANCED: Very stale baguette

EGG ROULETTE ★★

PLAYERS: 2–6

EGGINESS: 5

EQUIPMENT:

6 eggs per round

Lazy Susan (google what this is if you don't speak Chinese)

INSTRUCTIONS:

Hard boil five of the six eggs.

When cooled, place all six onto the Lazy Susan.

Spin the Lazy Susan so that no one knows where the fresh egg is.*

Players take it in turns to smash an egg onto their forehead. The loser is the one who smashes the fresh egg onto their forehead.**

* Two people with absolutely appalling memories could also play this without the need for the Lazy Susan.

** This can also be played using a large revolver designed for shooting bullets the size of eggs.

EGG FACT
Battery eggs will not power your vibrator.

EGG FACT
Free-range eggs are not free. Ask your local store detective to explain this after he's arrested you for shoplifting.

EGG FACT
Eggs can generally be found in all good supermarkets, but if not just go into the country and pick wild ones from an egg bush.

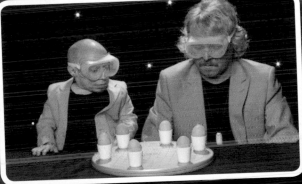

THE JAPANESE POPPADOM-SMASHING CHALLENGE ★★★★

If you hate poppadoms and love smashing things, then this game is for you.

PLAYERS:
2 teams, plus 1 umpire

EQUIPMENT:

At least 80 poppadoms

1 headband per player with Japanese logo

Stopwatch

Gong

The total absence of knowledge about world food

The belief that Japan is part of the Indian subcontinent

INSTRUCTIONS:

Set four stacks of ten poppadoms in a row on a table.

Put on the protective Japanese headband.

When the umpire bangs the gong and starts the stopwatch, begin headbutting the poppadom stacks.

When all the poppadoms are smashed, the umpire stops the clock.

Repeat for the other team.

The fastest team wins.

NB: For extra authenticity, play in a dojo.

WARNING!
May cause headaches

FOODSTUFFS THAT YOU SHOULD NOT ATTEMPT TO SMASH WITH YOUR HEAD:

Coconuts
Tinned sweetcorn
Crabs
Terry's Chocolate Orange
Jars of pickled eggs
Toffee apples
Rock cakes
Roast porcupine

29

CELEBRITY PIZZA FACE

★ ★ ★ ★ ★ ★ ★

PLAYERS: As many as you want, as long as they are not wheat-intolerant

EQUIPMENT:

Pizzas

Variety of pizza toppings

Wood-fired pizza oven*

DO NOT ATTEMPT TO EAT RAW PIZZA.

INSTRUCTIONS

Take a pizza, and using the variety of pizza toppings, make a portrait of a famous person on it.

Cook the pizza for 10–15 minutes at 220°C.

The other players have to guess the famous pizza face.

You win a point if they guess correctly. If they don't, eat the pizza and don't let them have any.

Jedward are always full of surprises, so we shouldn't have been surprised when, surprisingly, they turned out to be the Picassos of pizza! Here's the celebrity pizza face they made; can you guess who it is?

* If you don't have one in your back garden, ask Jamie Oliver if he'll let you use his. If he says no, just use your oven.

Here are some celebrity pizza faces we made earlier, can you tell who they are?

1

L _ _ Y / _ A _ A

2

_ R _ _ _ / _ _ V _ D

3

_ U _ _ _ / _ _ Y _ E

4

_ E _ _ A

5

_ O L _ _ / _ I _ L _ _ _ _ _ _

No, it was Emma Bunton. But you were close.*

* You weren't.

ANSWERS on the answers page p156

LADY GARGLE

This game was invented after one of the staff emerged from Keith's dressing room with an urgent need to gargle with TCP. As she gargled, it sounded like the opening bars to Franz Liszt's *Hungarian Rhapsody No. 2* – lo, Lady Gargle was born, slapped in the face and placed on the breast.

PLAYERS: At least 2, but the real Lady Gargle plays it with 20,000 people at the O2 Arena

EQUIPMENT:

Decorative refuse

Water

INSTRUCTIONS:

Using the decorative refuse, make your room look like Lady Gaga's bedroom: drape police tape everywhere, throw around some slabs of raw meat and shards of mirror, and fill the remaining available space with hats and lobsters. Cover your nipples with electrical tape.

Take a mouthful of water and gargle a popular song.

The first player to guess your song wins a point.

Repeat until you run out of songs or water, whichever's first.

* If you are allergic to water, use another liquid. Eg:

MILK
Milky

RUNNY EGG
Eggy

FAIRY LIQUID
Foamy

KETCHUP
Looks like you are dying from Ebola virus

IRN BRU
Popular amongst Scottish garglers

GUINNESS
Pour a pint and pretend it's petrol

BLUE WKD
Looks like you've sucked off a Smurf

Keith's headline:
'Pop star Rihanna is sick of being single, she wants a boyfriend to play with.'

Jason Donovan's interpretation: 'Ock schtaaa ee-anna ish shick of eeing shingle, she wants a oy-fren to eyay with.'

SPRAY WHAT?

In an ideal world, this is what the 10 O'Clock News would be like.

⭐⭐⭐

EQUIPMENT:

Newspaper

Mouth guard from a tooth-whitening kit

Waterproof garments

INSTRUCTIONS:

You put the mouth guard in your mouth. The other players put on the waterproof garments.

Read out a headline from the newspaper. If another player can work out what you're saying, they win a point.

Repeat until everybody is drenched in your spittle.

CELEBRITY THREESOMES ⭐⭐

Sorry to disappoint, but this is a word game. Your dreams involving you, Mark Wright and Kelly Brook will have to remain in your head.

EQUIPMENT:

Keep a thesaurus on standby

bang tidy (n.) paugu korrastada (Estonian): bang rangé (French): explosión ordenada (Spanish): düzenli patlama (Turkish)

INSTRUCTIONS:

Go to the toilet while the other players pick a celebrity, then come up with three words to describe them.

When you come out of the toilet (remember to wash your hands!), the other players tell you the three words. You have to guess which celebrity they've chosen.

Repeat until you've exhausted every combination of all the words in the English language, then try playing in other languages.

AND THE SCORES AT THE END OF THE GAMES ARE...

Sha-ting

CELEBRITY JUICE

CELEBRITY JUICE

CELEBRITY JUICE

....

write your scores here, you dingbat

HOW WELL DO YOU KNOW

?

Test your knowledge to find out.

1. What is the name of the show?

- ☐ a. *Celebrity Juice*
- ☐ b. *Celebrity Moose*
- ☐ c. *Celebrity Hoose*
- ☐ d. *Have I Got News For You*

2. What is the missing word in the following catchphrase: 'I'm off for a ___, I'll see you in two'?

- ☐ a. Colonoscopy
- ☐ b. Game of squash
- ☐ c. Bike ride
- ☐ d. Poo

3. In Series 8, what was the name of the magazine in the Cover Stories round?

- ☐ a. *Hot Lesbicans*
- ☐ b. *Hot Potato*
- ☐ c. *Hot Shit*
- ☐ d. *Closererer*
- ☐ e. *The Times Literary Supplement*

4. Of the following people, who has been on the show the most often?

- ☐ a. Verne Troyer
- ☐ b. Dave Berry
- ☐ c. Barack Obama
- ☐ d. Ronnie Corbett

5. Keith thinks Fearne has abnormally large...

- ☐ a. Testsicles
- ☐ b. Career expectations
- ☐ c. Toenails
- ☐ d. Nostrils

6. In Lemon Head, what is American for 'Sector'?

- ☐ a. Sect-ER
- ☐ b. Sect-AR
- ☐ c. Sect-OR
- ☐ d. Sect-UR

38

7. What is Keith's nickname for Holly?

☐ a. Holly Willoughbaby
☐ b. Holly Willoughbooby
☐ c. Holly Willoughbatty
☐ d. Holly Willyousuckmeoff

8. Shouting One Out takes place in which nightclub?

☐ a. Bang Tidy's
☐ b. Tallywhackers
☐ c. Vodka Fog
☐ d. Fearne's Fishy Pocket

9. Spud is what kind of animal?

☐ a. Hamster
☐ b. T-Rex
☐ c. Bulldog
☐ d. Party

10. Which year did Celebrity Juice first appear on your screens?

☐ a. 2007
☐ b. 2008
☐ c. 2009
☐ d. 1967

11. What colour does Keith say his hair is?

☐ a. Strawberry
☐ b. Blond
☐ c. Strawberry lond
☐ d. Ginger

12. What colour does Fearne say Keith's hair is?

☐ a. Strawberry
☐ b. Blond
☐ c. Strawberry blond
☐ d. Ginger

13. Which member of McFly did the general public think had the biggest tallywhacker?

☐ a. Danny
☐ b. Tom
☐ c. Harry
☐ d. Dougie

14. In Dappy Slapping what was the last thing Dappy got slapped in the face with?

☐ a. Massive dildo
☐ b. Paddle
☐ c. Fish
☐ d. Ginger wig

ANSWERS on the answers page p159

Get the
CELEBRITY JUICE
LOOK

By this point in the book you've been having a bloody great time playing Celebrity Juice at home. But deep down, you know that something's missing. You feel you don't quite look the part! Fortunately, there's an easy solution which involves no plastic surgery:

1. Put on a blonde wig.

2. Cut out these shapes.

3. Glue them on your mirror.

4. Look into your mirror and whaddayaknow, Keith, Holly and Fearne are looking back at you!

Holly's Willoughboobies

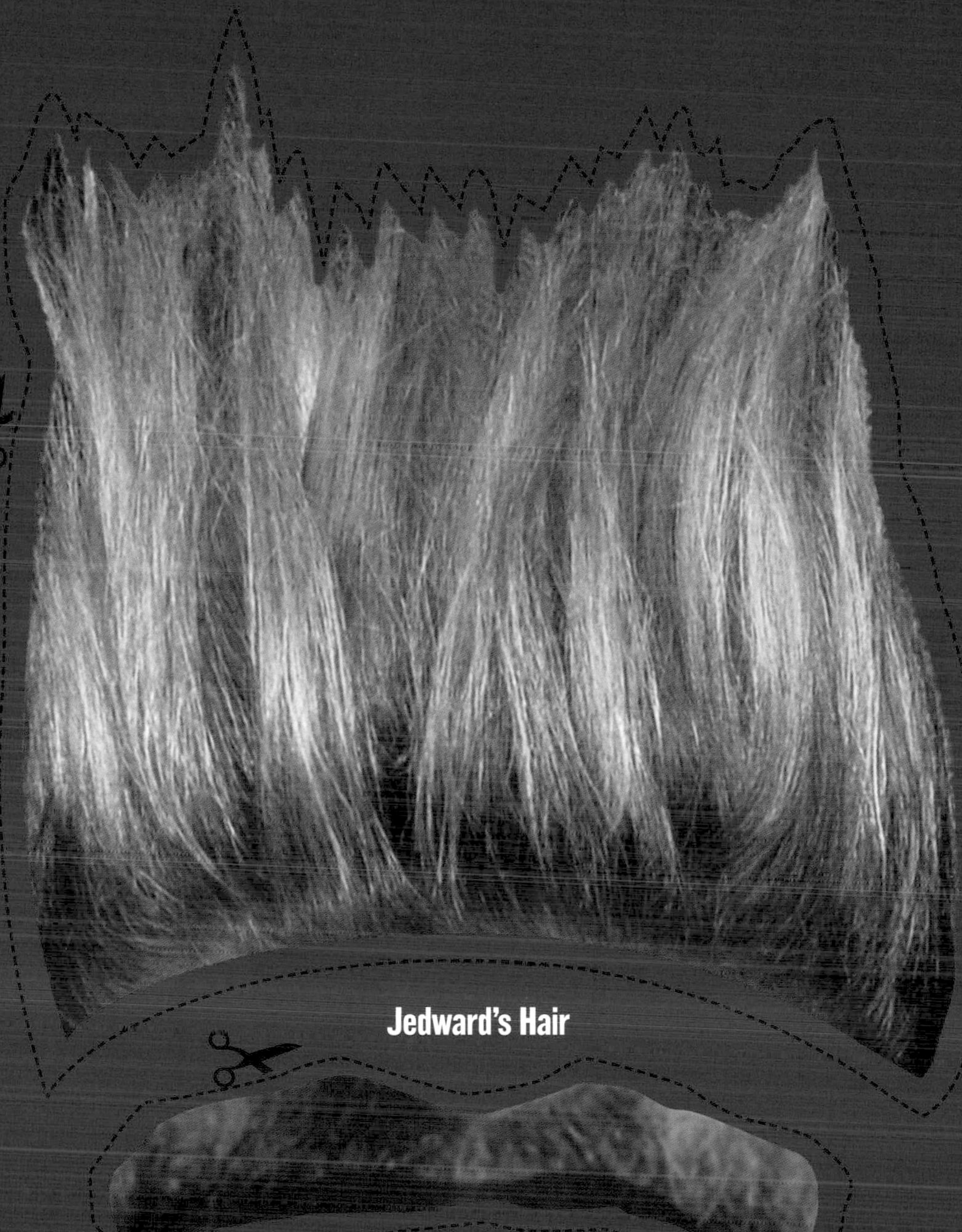

Jedward's Hair

Keith's Moustache

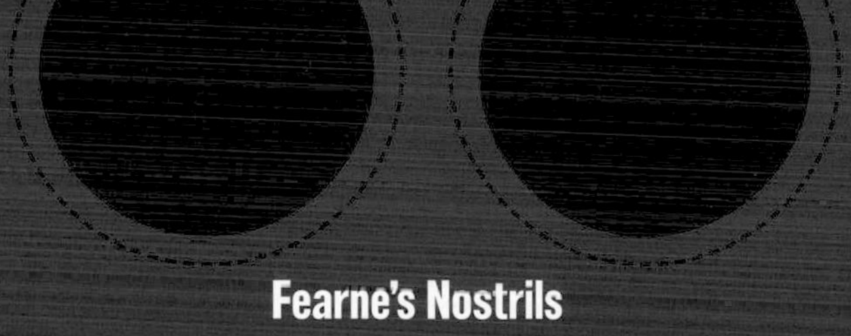

Fearne's Nostrils

41

Keith loves doggy style. Holly loves doggy style. Fearne loves doggy style. We all love doggy style! And now it's your turn to have some fun

Doggy STYLE

Can you guess the celebrity owner of these dressed-up doggies?

1
_O_ / C_T__N

2
T__ / Q__E_

3
_U__ / H___N

SPUD THE DOG

4

_ZZ_ / __B_____

5

_R / _

6

_I__I / M__A_

7

P__ / _U__H_R

8

_US____ / _R__D

9

JE_____

ANSWERS on the answers page p157

1

K____ / _R__K

2

__Y__C_

WHO ARE YOU KIDDING?

This is one of our favourite games on Celebrity Juice. The only problem is that it is impossible to beat Fearne Cotton at it, because she is an absolute ninja when it comes to recognising celebrities as babies.

You show her a muddy black and white photo of a 6-month-old baby with half of its face covered by its blanky, and Fearne will immediately tell you exactly who it is.

Joe Swash, on the other hand, wasn't quite so successful, mistaking a photo of the infant Jenson Button for… himself! Bravo, Joe, bravo.

Now you can test your own ability at this game. Below are childhood photos of 16 celebrities; can you guess who they are now they're all grown up?

3

A_A___ / H___E_

4

C___S / _V___

5

_ST__ / M__YG___

6

M___ / __R_L_

7

_A_____ / _____

ANSWERS on the answers page p157

You can't come on Celebrity Juice if you're not a celebrity. Chances are you're not a celebrity, but if you were a celebrity,

WHAT TYPE OF
CELEBRITY
WOULD YOU BE?

Take our quiz to find out, because you never know when celebrity is going to strike.

Exhausted by working for six weeks a year, you decide you need a break. Where do you go on holiday?

- [ ] a. Johnny Depp's private island in the Bahamas
- [ ] b. Simon Cowell's yacht in the Mediterranean
- [ ] c. Paul Danan's caravan in Tenby

Your favourite food is:

- [ ] a. Appetite-suppressing drugs
- [ ] b. Booze
- [ ] c. Iceland prawn vol-au-vents you stole from the buffet when you crashed Kerry Katona's birthday party

Despite an appalling track record with relationships, your massive ego wants to start a family, so you:

- [ ] a. Adopt a baby from an African country you can't even find on a map, then check in with the nanny every few months to make sure little Camelot Diamond is thriving in your care
- [ ] b. Give birth, just so you can get an 8-page spread in *TV Quick* featuring graphic photos of you in labour
- [ ] c. Stuff a pillow up your jumper and parade in front of the paparazzi, hoping the tabloids will go wild for your Secret Baby Joy. They don't. You try to claim child allowance for the pillow anyway

Which of these would be your holiday reading?

- [ ] a. Your own autobiography
- [ ] b. *Take a Break* magazine
- [ ] c. What's reading?

48

You are asked to be a guest judge on a talent show. You:

- ☐ a. Fail to turn up because you're on a three-day drug binge
- ☐ b. Cry through all the auditions and tell each contestant you want to be inside them
- ☐ c. Drunkenly get on stage halfway through an audition and try to sing 'Skyfall' by Adele

How do you get your pre-baby body back?

- ☐ a. Six hours a day in the gym, and a kelp juice cleanse
- ☐ b. Gastric band with lipo backup
- ☐ c. Smoke more heavily and switch to low-cal WKD

Which of these religions are you most drawn to?

- ☐ a. Scientology
- ☐ b. Church of England
- ☐ c. Derren Brown

HOW DID YOU SCORE?

MOSTLY A:
A-Lister
You are a bona fide A-lister! Enjoy your life of hedonism and unspeakable vacuity peppered with monumental levels of neediness and vanity.

MOSTLY B:
C-Lister
You're a C-lister. Your moderate level of fame will be counterbalanced by earning potential that is too small to sustain your lifestyle.

MOSTLY C:
Z-Lister
You are solidly Z-list and the only way is down. You could accept this fact and sign up for IT night classes, or you could keep praying for a comeback by making sure your sex tape is extra-deviant.

Spot the difference

Jedward have been part of the Celebrity Juice team since Series 3. Every now and again, they jump on their spaceship to go to Planet Jedward but the rest of the time, they're with us. Here they are – how many differences can you spot?

ANSWERS on the answers page p157

TOP 10 GREATEST MOUSTACHES OF ALL TIME

1. KEITH LEMON

2. CHARLIE CHAPLIN

3. SALVADOR DALI

4. TOM SELLECK

5. POIROT

6. BORAT

7. CAPTAIN HOOK

8. HULK HOGAN

9. EINSTEIN

10. RON BURGUNDY

51

MOP HUMPS!

All the guests we have on Celebrity Juice are brilliant, otherwise they wouldn't be on Celebrity Juice. But how do you decide the best one of all? Check out our handy Celebrity fact files and decide for yourself.

(In no way should this be confused with a popular card game that rhymes with 'mop humps'.)

ABBEY CROUCH

Category: Bang Tidy

Fanciability: OOOOOOOOOOOOSH!

Special skills: Playing ball games with tall people

Best moment: Dressing up as a sexy cat on the Halloween special

MICHELLE KEEGAN

Category: Bang Tidy

Fanciability: FAF

Special skills: Acting, bangers, downing dubious liquids

Best moment: Drinking a pint seasoned with Keith's special ingredient

RONAN KEATING

Category: Pop Star

Number one singles: 9

Special skills: Living on rollercoasters, duetting with Keith

Best moment: Being dragged along holding Holly's ankle

KIMBERLEY WALSH

Category: Bang Tidy

Fanciability: You would destroy it

Special skills: Dancing, singing, being Northern

Best moment: Dancing in Blame it on the Boogie

DANNY DYER

Category: Actor

Real name: Malcolm Smith

Height: 6 foot

Special skills: Cockney rhyming slang, swearing, spotting UFOs

Best moment: Showing his softer side while reading out a story in his pink fluffy jumper

VERNE TROYER

Category: Actor

Height: 2 foot 8 inches

Special skills: Stunts, pterodactyl impressions

Best moment: Lifting up an inflatable dinghy in Can Verne Lift

DAVID HASSELHOFF

Category: Actor

Height: 6 foot 4 inches

Special skills: Singing in German, running along beaches, talking to cars, freeing Eastern Europe from socialist oppression

Best moment: Being caught cheating in the Berlin Wall Challenge

EMMA BUNTON

Category: Pop Star

Number one singles: 9

Special skills: Dancing, singing, talking vagina

Best moment: Being tricked into kissing Keith in 'Mysterious Girl'

MCFLY

Category: Pop Star

Number one singles: 7

Special skills: Ballroom dancing, jungle survival, having lots of tattoos but still looking like nice young men you could take home to meet Grandma

Best moment: Having to rank themselves in order of appendage size

JEDWARD

Category: Pop Stars

Number one singles: 0

Special skills: Looking like each other. Not much else

Best moment: The Attack Dog Challenge

HENRY WINKLER

Category: TV Star

Catchphrase: Aaaaaaaayyyyyyyyy

Special skills: Being The Fonz – the actual Fonz. Also, giving double thumbs up

Best moment: Beating Keith at removing bras with one hand

GINO D'ACAMPO

Category: Hunk

Height: Unknown

Special skills: Cooking, pretending not to be from Yorkshire

Best moment: Managing to keep up an Italian accent for whole shows despite being from Sheffield

MARK WRIGHT

Category: Hunk

Height: 5 foot 11 inches

Special skills: Reality, pulling birds

Best moment: Trying to do his *TOWIE* accent while Keith has a go at him for going out with Michelle Keegan

HELEN FLANAGAN

Category: Soap Star

Height: 5 foot 3 inches

Special skills: She's got great things in front of her.

Best moment: Taking longer to find Australia on a map than it took Captain Cook in real life

TOP 10 FUNNIEST MOMENTS OF

10. HOLLY PLAYING SHOUTING ONE OUT FOR THE FIRST TIME

The message Holly had to pass on to the next contestant was, 'Caroline and Harry are getting back together. She loves his baby face.' Instead, Lady Willoughbooby very confidently turned to the person next to her and stated, 'Caroline and Harry are getting back together. She loves his p***s!' And thus Shouting One Out immediately became our favourite game.

9. RONAN KEATING AND KEITH SING A DUET

Ronan's duet with Keith on the classic pop song 'Life Is a Rollercoaster' was a special moment which will stay in people's hearts for centuries to come. Sixteen women got pregnant with twins just from watching it.

8. KEITH AS PUDSEY THE DOG

Keith and Ashley Roberts took on Ashleigh and Pudsey from *Britain's Got Talent* in a dog skills contest. Ashley and Pudsey JUST edged it. Just.

7. KEITH FALLING OVER WHILST GUNGING THOMAS TURGOOSE

The clip that lit up YouTube. Whilst gunging the losing team, (actor Thomas Turgoose, Fearne and Rufus Hound) Keith slipped over in his own gunge and was in a neck brace for a week.

6. THE SPRAY TAN CHALLENGE

The moment when Keith takes on Rylan in hosing down Jedward to give them a golden glow. No one likes to see Jedward writhe in pain being jetwashed with ice cold water on a freezing day. No hang on – that should read EVERYONE likes to see it.

TOP 10

5

5. KEITH'S LADY GAGA MEAT SUIT

Lady Gaga wore a meat dress. Keith went one better with a meat suit. The studio stank for days afterwards.

4. BRUNO AND MARVIN TAKE ON THE SUPERFAN

Strictly judge Bruno Tonoli and Marvin from JLS took on Juice superfan Gary Barlow, in a game of high stakes and deadly cunning. It ended up with Bruno looking like he'd been shat on. (It was just spaghetti sauce, don't worry.)

4

3

3. KEITH FALLING ON HIS NOSE IN BOOBY'S LAUNDRETTE

Keith tried to pick a photo of Fearne off the floor using only his mouth and fell head first onto his nose. Maybe it was funnier than it sounds on paper.

2. DANNY DYER BEING CALLED MALCOLM SMITH

Who's Danny Dyer? I know a Malcolm Smith but I've never heard of a Danny Dyer.

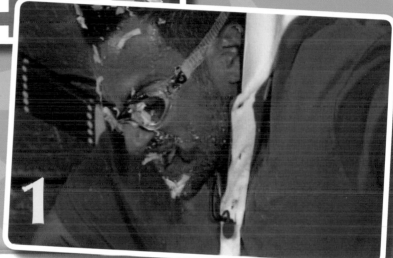

1. THE UPSIDE DOWN GAME

Peter Andre (he loves his kids, mate) looked like a right flamin' drongo when he went down under and had to make a kangaroo burger and got covered in tucker – strewth!

Those were OUR top 10 moments from Celebrity Juice, but what were YOUR top 10 moments from Celebrity Juice?

MY TOP 10 MOMENTS FROM CELEBRITY JUICE:

10. When Keith . . . .

9. The bit where . . . .

8. When Fearne . . . .

7. That thing which . . . .

6. When Spud the Dog . . . .

5. When Holly . . . .

4. The occasion when . . . .

3. The time when Keith's. . . . .

2. The second time when . . . .

1. When . . . .

PART 2

BODY POPPING ★★

INSTRUCTIONS:

Blow up balloons.

Get your breath back.

Stand opposite your teammate.

Place the inflated balloon in between your bodies.

The winning team is the one to pop the most balloons by hugging each other.

If that goes really well, maybe you will get to use one of those pickled onion condoms after all...

PLAYERS: Teams of 2

EQUIPMENT:

Packet of balloons*

* If you don't have balloons, use that job lot of cheap pickled onion-flavoured condoms you bought from that white van in the car park at Leicester Forest East services. Because face it, you're never going to get the chance to use them during sex.

14

60

IN YOUR FACE

In this game, Keith invites the panellists to stick their heads through the Incredible Hulk's anus. Not the real one – just a green screen with a hole cut out.*

PLAYERS: 2–20

TIME ALLOTTED:
An allotted time

EQUIPMENT:

Pen

Post-it notes

Keith then uses his most special effects to turn the panellist into another celebrity and they have to guess which one.

This is a great game to play at home, now that everybody's got a green screen and a lot of expensive professional-grade special effects equipment lying around. But if you lent yours to James Cameron and he hasn't given it back yet, you can still play In Your Face.

* Sorry if we just spoiled the magic.

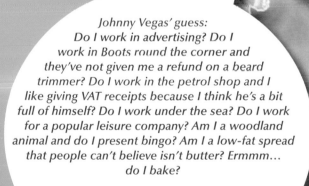

Johnny Vegas' guess:
Do I work in advertising? Do I work in Boots round the corner and they've not given me a refund on a beard trimmer? Do I work in the petrol shop and I like giving VAT receipts because I think he's a bit full of himself? Do I work under the sea? Do I work for a popular leisure company? Am I a woodland animal and do I present bingo? Am I a low-fat spread that people can't believe isn't butter? Ermmm… do I bake?

Keith: You were Paris Hilton.

Johnny: Oh it's so obvious when you say it.

INSTRUCTIONS:

Take the lid off the pen.

Use the pen to write the name of a celebrity on a Post-it note.

Stick the Post-it note onto another player's forehead.

The player may ask only yes or no questions to work out which celebrity they are.

If they haven't guessed correctly within the allotted time, the player has to change their legal name to the one on the Post-it.

63

TALK TO THE HAND BECAUSE THE FACE CAN'T MOVE ★★★

All the celebrities love a facelift. Give your friends the star treatment in the comfort of your own home.

PLAYERS: Several

EQUIPMENT:

Faces

Hands

Pair of welding gloves or marigolds

INSTRUCTIONS:

Choose one player to be the surgeon, and another to be the celebrity patient.

The surgeon puts on the gloves. The celebrity patient sits in a chair, awaiting their 'cosmetic refreshment'.

The surgeon stands behind the celebrity patient and stretches their face back in the style of a botched facelift.

The surgeon whispers an emotion into the celebrity patient's ear. The celebrity patient has to try to express the emotion upon their forever-young face.

The other players win a point if they can guess which emotion the celebrity patient is trying to convey.

HOLLY WILLOUGHBOOBY

I've always wanted to be the dragon from *The NeverEnding Story*

Here are some examples of players trying to master Talk To The Hand Because The Face Can't Move:

KATIE PRICE

I've just walked in on Alex Reid and Peter Andre in bed together

JONATHAN ROSS

Can I blow out the candles now?

CHRISTINE BLEAKLEY

I've just seen Frank Lampard naked in the shower

65

THE MOOB

This is a game that ITV's *The Cube* ripped off several years before we invented it. That scientific genius Pip Schofield must have built a time machine, travelled into the future, seen the Moob and copied it.

INSTRUCTIONS:

Construct a Moob-shaped frame using tentpoles and bamboo canes.

Cover it in Clingfilm.

Make a nipple out of a white T-shirt that turned pink when you accidentally put it through the hot wash with your new red towel.

Now you've got your very own Moob, play these games in it:

CELEBRITY EGGHEAD

Take a box of eggs and draw celebrities' faces on each egg. Dangle the box of eggs between your legs on a piece of rope, then swing it against a board until all the eggs are smashed.

BALANCE BEANS

Player 1 has to balance on a row of baked bean tins. Player 2 has to knock Player 1 off the tins by throwing a variety of beans at them.

ONE POTATO, TWO POTATO

Player 1 throws a bucket of potatoes on the floor. Player 2 has to count them in 10 seconds. Or else...

CELEBRITY BEAN FLICK

Flick your bean through the mouth of a cardboard cutout of a celebrity. Here's how Christine Bleakley did it:

BALLS DEEP

Tie a ball on a string onto your crotch. Squat over an open bottle and manoeuvre the ball into it.

FACEBALL

Throw a tennis ball at a wall three feet away. You win a point if it rebounds into your face.

DILDO HOOPLA

From a distance of 10 feet, throw a fastened bra and land it around a dildo.

SCOTCH EGG TELEPATHY

Player 1 eats a Scotch egg. Player 2, who is blindfolded, must shout when they think Player 1 has finished the Scotch egg. They win a point if they are correct to within three seconds.

CELEBRITEABAG

Attach a teabag to a swingball. Player 1 has to swing the teabag into Player 2's mouth. Here's Olly Murs teabagging Holly:

00:14

Don't be shy – wherever you are, whether you're on the bus, in an important work meeting, or having Sunday lunch with your gran, shout loud and proud:

I'M COMING!

★★★★ Embarrassed now? Well, you should be; that was a ridiculous thing to do. Stop being so suggestible.

If it's horrible, I will punch you!

I don't like this game, it's a horrible game.

This game is proof that everything is more fun when someone is wearing a blindfold. Just look at how much fun Fearne had playing I'm Coming!

Here's Gok Wan, faced with somebody who DOESN'T look good naked.

If you want to have as much fun as Fearne and Gok, here's how to play at home:

NUMBER OF PEOPLE: More than 4, fewer than the population of China

EQUIPMENT:

Blindfolds

A selection of disgusting household objects

EXAMPLES OF DISGUSTING HOUSEHOLD OBJECTS:

Clump of hair from the plughole

Recently used toilet brush

Your dad's stinking slippers

Sponge soaked with scummy washing-up water

Soiled nappy

Rotten bananas

Furry toy your cat sicked up

Squid

Bin juice

Cold spaghetti

Dirty underpants from the laundry basket

Margarine

Naked grandparent of your choice

INSTRUCTIONS:

Two players stand at one end of your living room wearing blindfolds. You stand at the other end. Between you and the two blindfolded dingbats stand three boxes, each containing two disgusting household objects.

Approach the first box and show the audience members (the remaining players, who are sat on your sofa) the disgusting household objects within. Whichever incites the loudest groan of disgust from the audience is the disgusting household object with which you will approach the increasingly nervous blindfolded contestants.

Grasping the disgusting household object, shout 'I'm Coming!' and advance towards the blindfolded contestants. If a contestant panics and removes their blindfold, they are out of the game and the other contestant wins a point. If a contestant manages to keep their blindfold on until you start stroking them with the disgusting household object, they win a point.

Repeat with the other two boxes, or until everybody refuses to play any more.

It really is as simple as peas.

THE WANTED LIST

70

THE WANTED LIST ✶✶

We played THE WANTED LIST with a particular band on the show. Can you guess which band it was? We WANTED them, and you really really WANTED them.

Oh come on, it's not that hard. No – it's not a band called the LIST. That's not the answer we WANTED... That's right, the band was THE WANTED! Jesus. You frikkin' dingbats. Anyway, here's how you play The Wanted List at home:

DIFFICULTY: 2, unless your rental contract states you're not allowed to put posters up, in which case 10

TIME ALLOTTED:
An allotted time

EQUIPMENT:

At least 30 posters of The Wanted

Blu-Tack

Household objects

INSTRUCTIONS:

Put up posters of The Wanted until the whole room is covered.

Behind each poster of The Wanted, hide one household object.

The players have to retrieve the household objects from behind The Wanted posters.

The winner is the player who retrieves the most household objects in the allotted time.

If you're not sure what a household object is, try using some of these:

Adult toy	Shoes
Deep-pan pizza	Ice cream
Moustache trimmings	Damp towel
Bar of soap	Your dad's car keys
Wooden leg	Salad
Dog	Cup of tea
The postman	

TALK THE PLANK ★★★★★

DIFFICULTY: 5,
10 if you can't swim

PLAYERS:

Minimum 2, maximum
a swimming pool-full

EQUIPMENT:

Swimming pool with
10m-diving board

INSTRUCTIONS:

Jump off the diving board and describe a celebrity as you hurtle towards the water. The other players have to guess the celebrity.

You have a maximum of three dives in which to describe the celebrity.

If you do not happen to have a swimming pool with a 10m-diving board, you can also play this game at home. Stand outside the house, and get the other player to pour a bucket of water onto your head from the upstairs window. You have to describe the celebrity before your head gets wet. Repeat with two more buckets of water if necessary.

This is the best game ever!

Don't be such a planker!

WARNING!
⚠
Don't drown
Don't break a rib
Don't get in Tom Daley's way
Don't play if the swimming pool has
   been drained for cleaning
Don't play in open water

As you can see, we're in Sweden! Inventors of Abba, Ikea, Abba, Ikea…

SWEDISH HOT TUB DRESS-UP CHALLENGE

★ ★ ★ ★

4, rising to 7 once your fingers go pruney

4, plus one wardrobe assistant

1 hot tub

3-piece suit, tie, shirt, socks, shoes, bowler hat – 1 of each

INSTRUCTIONS:

The players sit naked (or in their pants) in the hot tub.

The wardrobe assistant throws each player an item of clothing. Once the player has put it on, they receive the next item of clothing.

The winner is the player who is fully dressed first.

The real winner is the player who manages to get a good look under the water at everyone else's tallywhackers and tuppences.

STICKY BITS ★★★★★

This game is like the old party favourite Pin the Tail on the Donkey, but loads better because you play with a celebrity's face rather than a donkey's hairy bum! But if you want to recreate that retro flavour, you could play with a celebrity face that looks like a donkey's hairy bum.

WARNING!
Before you start to play, move the coffee table out of the way so that the players don't bang their shins on it. Also make sure there are no trip wires, lit barbecues or open manholes nearby

PLAYERS: 1 at a time, or it's carnage

EQUIPMENT:

Blindfold

Big picture of a celebrity's face with one of their features missing

The celebrity's missing facial feature

Blu-Tack

INSTRUCTIONS:

Stick the picture of the celebrity on the wall. Put blobs of Blu-Tack on the back of the celebrity's missing facial feature.

Let the player have a good look at the picture, then blindfold them. If you don't have a blindfold, make them wear a top hat that is far too big for them.

Stand the player a few feet away from the celebrity picture, place the facial feature in their hand, and give them a gentle shove in the direction of the picture on the wall.

If the blindfolded player can stick the facial feature in the correct place on the celebrity face, they win a point!

For a deluxe version of this game, see if a real live celebrity is willing to shave off their eyebrows then let you stick eyebrow wigs onto their face.

To help you get the hang of Sticky Bits, can you match the missing facial feature with the right famous face?

ANSWERS
on the answers page
p158

IT'S NOT THE OPPOSITE NAME GAME ✶

DIFFICULTY: 1–10, depending upon your capacity for abstract thought

PLAYERS: You, plus some others because this game does not work if you play it alone

EQUIPMENT:

Pen

Cards

Ability to write

This page

Watch, or similar time-keeping device*

* If you don't have one, ask a friend to shout out of the window, 'What's the bloody time?' Then when someone answers, continue shouting 'What's the bloody time?' until another passerby shouts back a time that is a minute later than the first time shouted.

INSTRUCTIONS:

Look below at the names of celebrities and pop groups but written in opposites.

Use the pen to write down on cards each of the 'opposites'.

Sit opposite the other player and show them each card in turn. They have one minute to guess as many opposites as they can.

Repeat with as many other players as you can find. The one who guesses the most opposites is the opposite of the loser.

Mrs Coffee	Mr T
East Death	Westlife
Skinny Lass Chunky	Fat Boy Slim
Night DVD Minge Out Daughter	David Dickinson*
Small Jill Woman	Hugh Jackman**
Yank Elbow Bullets	Britney Spears***
Elevator	Steps
Queens of Truth	Kings of Leon****
Sane Off Him	Madonna*****
Table Aberystwyth Gas	Cheryl Cole******
Girl Poor-ie	Guy Ritchie
Won't Jones	Will Smith
Gloss Night Lady	Matt Damon*******
White Eared Beans	Black Eyed Peas
Stiff Cake	Limp Bizkit

* Day Vid Dick In Son
** Huge Jack Man
*** Brit Knee Spears
**** Kings of Lying

***** Mad On Her
****** Chair Rhyl Coal
******* Matt Day Man

BOOBY'S LAUNDRETTE ★★★★★

Play this game in whichever room you keep the washing machine, unless you're a dingbat who keeps the washing machine on the roof, in which case play the game somewhere safe at ground level.

AGILITY: 4

EQUIPMENT:

Several empty boxes in a range of sizes*

1 mouth per player

* But make sure the smallest one is not so small that you could swallow it by accident.

INSTRUCTIONS:

Place the largest box in the middle of the floor.

Each player takes it in turns to pick up the box using only their mouth.

If the player cannot pick up the box with their mouth, or if their hands touch the ground, they are eliminated.

Repeat with the next largest box, and again until the very smallest box.

The last player standing wins a point, and a voucher for four sessions of physio.

WARNING!
Do NOT play this game if you have a bad back; go and have a nice sit down instead

Once you've mastered the boxes, you could play this game with:

Russian dolls

Contents of the fruit bowl

Hard-boiled eggs, from ostrich to quail

Shoes, preferably not ones you've worn on a walk through a muddy field

Plastic cups

Balloons

Cuddly toys

Star Wars figurines, from Chewbacca to Yoda

77

THE SHAWSHANK REDEMPTION DIDN'T DO VERY WELL AT THE CINEMA BUT DID DO QUITE WELL ON VHS ESCAPE FROM CARDBOARD BOX CHALLENGE

The SRDDVWATCBDDQWOVEFCB Challenge, for short.

PLAYERS: Minimum 2 prisoners, plus 1 prison warden

TIME: Less than 19 years, if you're lucky

EQUIPMENT:

1 large cardboard box per player, big enough to enclose an adult human fully

1 poster of Rita Hayworth* per player

Packing tape

Scissors

Siren

INSTRUCTIONS:

Prepare the cardboard boxes by using the scissors to cut a small barred window into one side. NB: If you can't be trusted to play safely with scissors, ask a grown-up to do this for you.

Stick up the Rita Hayworth poster inside the box.

Each prisoner gets into their box, then the prison warden seals up all the boxes with packing tape.

When the prison warden sounds the siren, each prisoner has to escape from their box.

The winner is the first person to break out and reach the beach in Mexico.

* If you don't fancy Rita Hayworth, use a poster of Kelly Brook.

AND THE SCORES AT THE END OF THE GAMES ARE...

Sha-ting

CELEBRITY JUICE

CELEBRITY JUICE

CELEBRITY JUICE

....
write your scores here,
you dingbat

START

You look **BANG TIDY** today. **THROW AGAIN.**

Cut out your counters and get ready to play.

KEITH

HOLLY

FEARNE

INDIAN KEITH

SPUD

Jodie Marsh gets a tattoo of your face. **START AGAIN.**

KATIE PRICE wants to marry you. **GO BACK 4.**

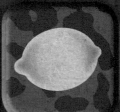

Someone mistakes you for a member of One Direction and won't serve you at the bar. **GO BACK 2.**

KATIE PRICE is divorcing you. GO FORWARD 2.

*Though we're still hoping that a manufacturer will produce it in time for next Christmas. We've had a definite maybe from the Ukrainian division of Waddingtons.

You win **REAR OF THE YEAR.** Let all the other players feel your bum, then **THROW AGAIN.**

You win **FIRST PRIZE** in a motting contest. **THROW AGAIN.**

Kelly Brook jogs past. **MISS A TURN** while your boner goes down.

Your YouTube dance goes viral. **THROW AGAIN.**

Someone mistakes you for a member of One Direction and wants to shag you. **GO FORWARD 3.**

SPUD THE DOG pisses on your new snakeskin shoes – **GO BACK 2.**

If you're wearing leopard print, **THROW AGAIN**

CELEBRITY JUICE

CELEBRITY JUICE *The* **BOARD GAME** NOT AVAILABLE IN THE SHOPS!*

HAPPY FINISH

You are offered a place in the Celebrity Juice magazine. **MISS 2 TURNS.**

The Hoff gives you driving lessons. **GO FORWARD 2.**

You walk in on SuBo taking a shower. **GO BACK 3.**

You get out of a car without flashing your pants. **MISS A TURN.**

IS VERNE BIGGER THAN?

Bonsai Tree

Guitar

Peter Crouch

Gary the dog

Jodie Marsh's arm

Traffic Light

Club sandwich

Complete works of Dickens

Tom Cruise

Digestive Biscuit

Pint of beer

Ant

82

VERNE IS BIGGER THAN...

See the items on the opposite page?
Place them on the graph in order
of height.

| 1 | 2 | 3 | 4 | 5 | 6 | | 7 | 8 | 9 | 10 | 11 | 12 |

ANSWERS on the answers page p157

HOW WELL DO YOU KNOW

CELEBRITY JUICE ?

Take our quiz to find out.

3. Which celebrity kept Fearne Cotton's team captain seat warm when she went off and had a baby?

- ☐ a. Kelly Brook
- ☐ b. The Queen
- ☐ c. Jedward
- ☐ d. Cat Woman

1. Which famous children's character does Keith always compare Stacey Solomon to?

- ☐ a. Minnie Mouse
- ☐ b. Rasta Mouse
- ☐ c. Felix The Cat
- ☐ d. Danger Mouse

4. What did Keith reveal he kept in his wallet while playing Booby's Laundrette?

- ☐ a. Picture of himself
- ☐ b. Picture of Fearne Cotton
- ☐ c. Picture of Holly Willoughbooby
- ☐ d. Picture of his tallywhacker

2. Which Celebrity Juice panellist has the following lyrics in one of his tracks: 'Holly Willoughby, you can come and run my bath'?

- ☐ a. Tinie Tempah
- ☐ b. Tinchy Stryder
- ☐ c. Tulisa
- ☐ d. Eminem

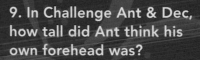

5. Which of the celebrities below has not appeared in the VT round?

- [ ] a. The Hoff
- [ ] b. Rylan Clark
- [ ] c. Verne Troyer
- [ ] d. Peter Andre

6. Which of the following celebrities did Keith pretend to mott out?

- [ ] a. Jeremy Clarkson
- [ ] b. Phillip Schofield
- [ ] c. Jerry Springer
- [ ] d. Olly Murs

7. What did Dec from Ant and Dec say his favourite sexual position is?

- [ ] a. Basset Hound
- [ ] b. Reverse Cowgirl
- [ ] c. Big Dipper
- [ ] d. Deep Impact

FOR A BONUS POINT: Did Ant guess it correctly?

- [ ] a. Yes
- [ ] b. No

8. Which Superhero did Verne Troyer help Keith impersonate in the Lemon Head round?

- [ ] a. Superman
- [ ] b. Iron Man
- [ ] c. Spider-Man
- [ ] d. The Hulk

9. In Challenge Ant & Dec, how tall did Ant think his own forehead was?

- [ ] a. 6 centimetres
- [ ] b. 5 centimetres
- [ ] c. 30 centimetres
- [ ] d. 2 metres

10. How tall was Ant's forehead?

- [ ] a. 5 centimetres
- [ ] b. 6 centimetres
- [ ] c. 11 centimetres
- [ ] d. 25 centimetres

11. In Keith's romantic book, *Strawberry Blond*, what was the main character called?

- [ ] a. Heath Lime
- [ ] b. Peter Rabbit
- [ ] c. John Major
- [ ] d. Simon Cowell

12. What is Keith's sign-off to each show?

- [ ] a. If I don't see ya through the week, I'll see ya through the window
- [ ] b. Nice to see you...to see you nice!
- [ ] c. You are the weakest link, goodbye
- [ ] d. Our survey says...

ANSWERS on the answers page p156

COCKWORD

ACROSS

1. Penis (3,5)
6. Penis (7)
7. Penis (5)
8. Penis (4)
11. Penis (6)
12. Penis (4)
13. Penis (4,7)
16. Penis (7,5)
19. Penis (4)
20. Penis (4)
21. Penis (4)

DOWN

1. Penis (4,7)
2. Penis (6,4)
3. Penis (6,6)
4. Penis (7.6)
5. Penis (4)
9. Penis (9)
10. Penis (6-6,6)
14. Penis (4,9)
15. Penis (7,6)
16. Penis (12)
17. Penis (3,4)
18. Penis (4,5)

DOT-TO-DOT

WHAT'S IN MY MCFLY?

Can you guess what the McFly boys are hiding in their trousers?

T _ _ M _ _ _

_ _ D G _ _

SC _ _ _ _ N _ V _ _

B _ _ U _ TT _ /
G _ _ L _ C

ANSWERS
on the answers page
p158

Spot the GOLDEN POTATO

Once every 2000 years, an Irish potato farmer manages to grow a golden potato and is crowned the Golden Potato King. In exchange for 80% of the Celebrity Juice annual budget, we managed to acquire one of these golden potatoes, and thus the game Spot The Golden Potato was born.

On the show, the teams have to spot the differences Keith has made to the studio when the lights are turned down, and they win 10 bonus points if they spot the Golden Potato. But it can be an elusive little critter: so far it has hidden in a nail salon, a pub and in a cinema watching *Friends With Benefits*. The Golden Potato can't resist a romcom.

But let's not allow the Celebrity Juice panellists to have all the potato-spotting fun – you too can play along at home with this activity, as we have a hidden a golden potato* somewhere in this book. You will win 10 points for your team (that lives in your head) if you can spot it.

So point your eyes at this book and see if you can spot the Golden Potato. It could be anywhere, it could be on page 12,** it could be on page 24,*** it could even be on page 69.****

Remember, you don't get any points for spotting normal potatoes so don't get caught out! Good luck with your potato hunting, Potato Hunters, and may the Potato Gods be ever in your favour.

Potato!

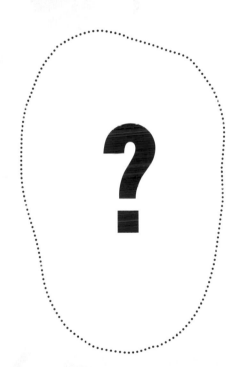

* A picture of one, don't be a dingbat.
** It's not.
*** It's not.
**** It's not (69, tec hee).

SUPERCOMPUTER K.L.I.T.

DEL-EAT MY SPAM | JESSIE J PEGS | ANGRY BIRDS OR HORNEY BIRDS | RANDOM ROUND

10 ▪ 001 ▪ 111 ▪ 101

1001

K EITH
L EMON
I NFORMATION
T ECHNOLOGY

Facts

☐ SUPERCOMPUTER K.L.I.T. IS THE MOST ADVANCED COMPUTER IN THE WORLD.

☐ SUPERCOMPUTER K.L.I.T. HAS A KECAGAZZILIOBYTE OF RAM.

☐ THE SUPERCOMPUTER K.L.I.T. DELUXE BUNDLE INCLUDES HD WEBCAM, WIRELESS MOUSE AND WINDOWS 97.

KEITH
LEMON
INFORMATION
TECHNOLOGY

If you don't have NASA's budget to buy SUPERCOMPUTER K.L.I.T., you can build your own SUPERCOMPUTER K.L.I.T. at home:

PHASE 1: GET A CARDBOARD BOX.

PHASE 2: FILL THE CARDBOARD BOX WITH GREEN JELLY.

PHASE 3: WHEN THE JELLY IS SET, TEAR OFF ONE OF THE SIDES OF THE BOX.

PHASE 4: SHOVE YOUR HEAD INTO THE BOX.

PHASE 5: LIGHT YOURSELF FROM BENEATH WITH A TORCH.

PHASE 6: TWEAK YOUR NIPPLES TO ADJUST YOUR VOLUME AND SCREEN BRIGHTNESS.

YOU ARE NOW READY TO PROCESS VAST AMOUNTS OF INFORMATION.

☐ SUPERCOMPUTER K.L.I.T. CONTAINS A HYPERCHARGED DYNAMIC P3N15 Pentium PROCESSOR, CAPABLE OF MAKING MORE THAN THREE CALCULATIONS A MINUTE.

☐ SUPERCOMPUTER K.L.I.T. CAN DO ALL THE TIMES TABLES SIMULTANEOUSLY AND RECITE π TO TWO DECIMAL PLACES.

☐ SUPERCOMPUTER K.L.I.T.'S CELEBRITY CRUSH IS CAROL VORDERMAN.

ANSWERS on the answers page p158

WHAT'S MY NAHHHHHAME?

Oh no – SUPERCOMPUTER K.L.I.T. has malfunctioned! The files containing celebrities and horses have become corrupted and SUPERCOMPUTER K.L.I.T. has combined the celebrities with the horses. Can you guess these celebrities' nahhhhhhhames?

__SS__L / B___D

L___ / _A_A

__M / CR___E

Error [×]

❌ **K.L.I.T RED ALERT**

SYSTEM ERROR c:/80085
Please change the fuseses

[RESTART]

ANSWERS
On the answers page
p15g

WHO'S BEEN RAMMED?

Oh no – SUPERCOMPUTER K.L.I.T. has malfunctioned again and the files it was storing which contained celebrities and rams have now become corrupted too (really need to get those fuses fixed). SUPERCOMPUTER K.L.I.T. has combined the celebrities with the rams, so can you work out which celebrities have been rammed?

__ST__ / B___E_

J___M_ / _LA__S__

_NG__I__ / J__I_

THE FOLLOWING COMMERCIALLY AVAILABLE GAMES ARE ALSO COMPATIBLE WITH SUPERCOMPUTER K.L.I.T.'S OPERATING SYSTEM:

Titris

Mortal Cumbat

Dogger

Turds with Friends

Biocock

Masturbation Hero

Draw Nothing

Cock Band

Half-Wife 2

Wee Fit

Resident Weevil 2

Angry Balls

Championship Regional Manager

Super Street

Sweeper 2

Weston-super Mario

Knob of War 3

Tekken from Behind

Pro Evolution Swingball

Call of Booty: Black Plops

HAVE FUN PLAYING WITH YOUR K.L.I.T

95

Joey Essex

THE QUIZ

We at Celebrity Juice love Joey Essex. We love him for his face, but we love him even more for his brain, which works in a completely different way to every other brain we have ever met.

Twice on the show we asked him the following question:

Which country borders Wales?

The first time, his answer was 'London'. Could've been worse – London is a place in the UK, just not a country. Or next to Wales. So we told him the correct answer was England. Which it is.

When we asked him the same question a few months later, his answer was...Russia. An improvement – at least this time it was a country. Though still not very near Wales.

Joey came back on the show recently, and you guessed it, he answered it correctly. As you can tell, Joey's making really good progress, and you can help him keep that up: if you bump into Joey around Essex, test him with a question from our quiz.

1. How many legs does a spider have?

a. 8
b. 500
c. 4 wheels

2. What are the three emergency services?

a. Vajazzle artist, tooth bleacher, hair straightener
b. Ambulance, police, fire service
c. Cubs, brownies, girl guides

3. What are Ugg Boots made of?

a. Sheepskin
b. Ugly people
c. Bread

4. What kind of fuel do you put in a diesel car?

a. Coal
b. Ribena
c. Diesel

5. What is the correct name for a baby swan?

a. Nigel
b. Mr Swan
c. Cygnet

6. Where is the ozone layer?

a. Under the sofa
b. In the Earth's atmosphere
c. In your pants

7. What do you do when the lightbulb has blown?

a. Change the lightbulb
b. Run around screaming 'I've gone blind, I've gone blind!'
c. Move house

8. Which country borders Wales?

a. Japan
b. England
c. The moon

9. Who are Richard and Judy?

a. Adam and Eve
b. Stars from the telly
c. The people who created the world

10. Who is this?

a. Member of the Osbourne family
b. Pop star
c. Gino D'Acampo's dad

ANSWERS on the answers page p159

FAVOURITE
MAGAZINE GUESTS

Our personal highlight of every episode of Celebrity Juice* is the mystery magazine guest, just as the highlight of the life of every mystery magazine guest is to stand within the pages of that hallowed magazine, and feel the ashes of their near-forgotten fame being fanned back into life for up to 30 seconds.**

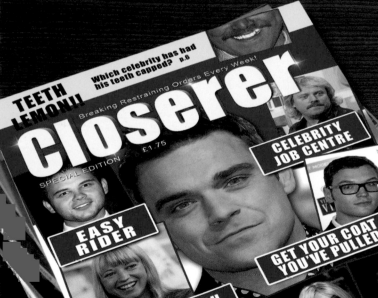

* After Keith, Holly, Fearne, the guests, the games, the VT rounds, the bit where Keith kicks the @CelebJuice sign, and the rest.

** 30 seconds may be reduced to 0 seconds in the edit.

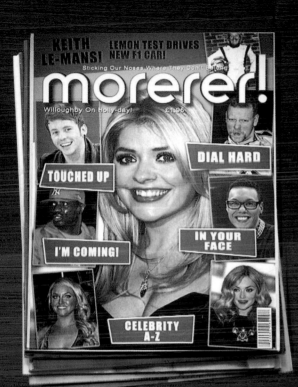

KEITH LE-MANS! **LEMON TEST DRIVES NEW F1 CAR!**

Sticking Our Noses Where They Don't Belong

morerer!

Willoughby On Holly-day! £1.96

TOUCHED UP

DIAL HARD

I'M COMING!

IN YOUR FACE

CELEBRITY A-Z

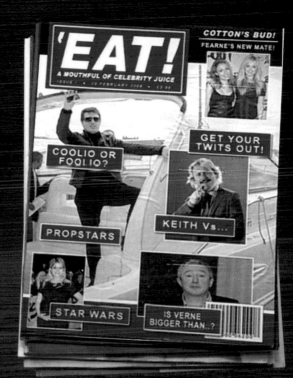

COTTON'S BUD! **FEARNE'S NEW MATE!**

'EAT!

A MOUTHFUL OF CELEBRITY JUICE

ISSUE 1 • 20 FEBRUARY 2008 • £2.99

GET YOUR TWITS OUT!

COOLIO OR FOOL IQ?

KEITH Vs...

PROPSTARS

STAR WARS

IS VERNE BIGGER THAN..?

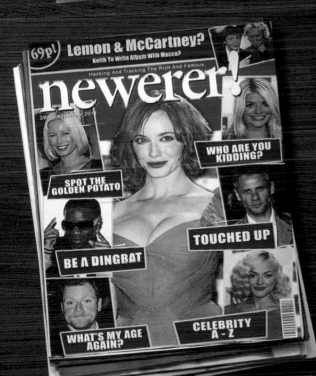

69p! **Lemon & McCartney?**

Keith To Write Album With Macca?

Hacking And Tracking The Rich And Famous

newerer!

29th September 2011

SPOT THE GOLDEN POTATO

WHO ARE YOU KIDDING?

BE A DINGBAT

TOUCHED UP

WHAT'S MY AGE AGAIN?

CELEBRITY A - Z

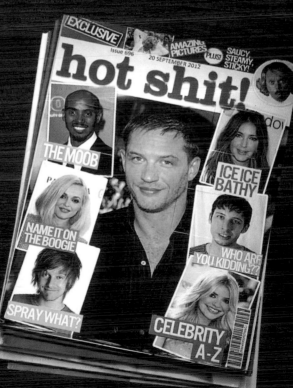

EXCLUSIVE

Issue 696 • 20 SEPTEMBER 2012

AMAZING PICTURES PLUS! **SAUCY, STEAMY, STICKY!**

hot shit!

THE MOOB

ICE ICE BATHY

NAME IT ON THE BOOGIE

WHO ARE YOU KIDDING??

SPRAY WHAT?

CELEBRITY A-Z

99

 TOP **10**

10. GILLIAN MCKEITH

Legend of faecal health. She didn't do much on the show, but she did have a good old rummage through Keith, Holly and Fearne's poo after the show. Holly needs to eat more fibre apparently.

IN YOUR FACE

9

9. THE CHUCKLE BROTHERS

Legends of physical comedy and saying 'To me, to you, to me, to you, to me, to you, to me, to you, to me, to you, to me, to you (is this enough yet?).'

8. PETER DICKSON

Legendary voice of *The X Factor*. Thrilled the panel by saying all their names as if introducing them on *The X Factor*. Then billed us for each one afterwards. Cheque's in the post, Peter!

X-Factor ...al £1.75

8

PARIS STILTON

7. HUNTER

Legend from *Gladiators*.
Lifted comedian Chris
Ramsey over his head.

6. THE CHEEKY GIRLS

Legends of cheekiness.
The best thing to come out
of Transylvania since Count
Duckula.

TOP 10

5. LEMBIT OPIK

Legendary Lib Dem who used to shag one half of number 6. He's the only MP who has ever been on the show. Possibly the only MP who's ever even heard of the show.

4. SCOTT ROBINSON FROM 5IVE

Boyband legend from legendary boyband 5ive. Afterwards he taught JLS the dance moves to 5ive's 1999 chart-topping* hit 'If Ya Gettin' Down'.

3. LOU CARPENTER

Aussie soap legend. The longest-serving character in *Neighbours*, since he backed his car over Bouncer.

* In New Zealand.

JUST LIKE
TARS

2. WAGNER

The legendary *X Factor* contestant and retired PE teacher showed Keith exactly how he'll look like in thirty years.

1. ROLAND RAT

Legendary rat. Though the majority of the audience mistook him for Stacey Solomon.

We've been making Celebrity Juice for ITV2 since 2008, but our ancestors have been making it for a lot longer than that.

THROUGH THE AGES

65000000 BC

'And the scores at the end of that round are RAAAAAARRRR!'

2500 BC

33 AD

'That's a point for Judas's team!'

XEVNT:CABALII   DENAVIBVS · - E

1066 AD

'Opposite adjacent to me is a massive Bayeux! Tapestry.'

1547 AD

'I would smash your back Tudoors in.'

'I would smash your Bach doors in.'

1730 AD

106

1815 AD

'I'm off to Waterloo, I'll see you in two.'

1922 AD

107

1966 AD

'It's now time to play Twist and Shouting One Out'

1986 AD

'Next up it's the VHS round.'

2008 AD

'My name's Keith Lemon and welcome to Celebrity Juice!'

2313 AD

'1000101111100101010101011111010100111110010.'

PART
3

SILENCE OF THE LAMBS ✴

INSTRUCTIONS:

Two players, one from each team, sit opposite each other.

Player 1 must maintain a straight face to win a point for their team.

Player 2 may use insults, jokes and physical comedy to win a point for their team by making Player 1 smile or laugh.

For practice, try to raise a smile from father and son Larry Lamb and George Lamb below.

DIFFICULTY: 1–10

PLAYERS: 2 teams

EQUIPMENT:
Ingenuity

TIPS TO MAINTAIN A STRAIGHT FACE:

- Have extensive botox
- Stick your face in the freezer for half an hour beforehand
- Attach weights to your jowls
- Think about poor little puppies out in the cold

OTHER FAMOUS PARENTS AND THEIR KIDS:

Trevor McDonald and his
daughter Jane McDonald

Anne Robinson and her son
Johnny Robinson

Spencer Matthews and his dad
Bernard Matthews

Derren Brown and his mum
June Brown

Michelle Keegan and her dad
Kevin Keegan

Mark Wright and his dad
Ian Wright

Adrian Chiles and his daughter
Amy Childs

Carol Vorderman and her dad
Lord Voldemort

Will Smith and his mum
Dame Maggie Smith

LEMON HEAD ✸✸

Wait! Stop chopping off your own head to replace it with a lemon – there's an easier way to play Lemon Head, and this is it:

NUMBER OF PLAYERS: Everyone, divided into 2 teams

TIME ALLOTTED: An allotted time

EQUIPMENT:

Headlines, pictures, VTs, props or tweets relating to a topical celebrity story

Keith's head below*

INSTRUCTIONS:

Each team takes it in turns to choose a sector from Keith's head.

According to their choice, the team receives a headline, picture, VT, prop or tweet that is a clue to a topical celebrity story.

If they successfully guess the story, they win a point.

The winning team is the team that wins.

STILL NOT SURE HOW LEMON HEAD WORKS?

On the page opposite there is an example of a topical celebrity story that would be suitable for Lemon Head if it was true (which it isn't, because we made it up for demonstration purposes).

* If more convenient, use your grandad's head: while he's snoozing in his chair in front of the snooker, use a marker pen to draw the categories on his face.

The Daily Rag

Voted Britain's Best Ever Newspaper

VICTORIA BECKHAM IS EXPECTING TWINS WITH WILL.I.AM

PLEASE NOTE: This picture has been Photoshopped because this never happened. It is a story we made up. We cannot emphasise that enough.

She isn't, but if she was – which she isn't, because we made this story up – here are clues you could use to play Lemon Head:

HEADLINE:
Posh and Pea Produce a Pair

PICTURE:
A baby scan where the two foetuses look like baby versions of Posh and Will.I.Am

VT:
Keith, dressed as Posh, is in hospital giving birth. The doctor, also played by Keith, would pull out two babies, one black and one white. He would hand them to Keith, dressed as Will.I.Am, who would say something like, "This is dope!"

PROP:
A big chair like on The Voice spins round to reveal Keith dressed as Posh, breastfeeding two babies.

TWEET:

Victoria Beckham @poshspice
@williamBEPeas it's your turn to change the nappies lol!

113

Grab your balls, stretch your groin muscles and get ready to be sweaty – the whistle has blown for the

CELEBRITY JUICE

SPORTS
DAY

Gather together several players. Anyone who claims they can't play because they've got a bad leg can sit and watch, but ONLY if they have a note from Matron.

Each player will need to be wearing the proper kit of sweatbands and side-vent short shorts. If anybody leaves their kit at home, they will have to play in their vest and pants.

One of you gets to be umpire, for which you will need a shiny tracksuit, a whistle, and the ability to shout humiliating remarks to anyone who's a bit slow and/or chubby.

You will also need a selection of trophies to award the victors. If you can't get any from the charity shop, coat some kitchen utensils in gold spray-paint.

READY... SET... GO!

CHICKEN AND SPOON RACE

PLAYERS: Probably gets a bit messy if there are more than 6 of you per heat

EQUIPMENT:

1 spoon per player

1 chicken per player*

Like the egg and spoon race for grown-ups.

INSTRUCTIONS:

Players line up at the start of the race track and place the chickens carefully on the spoons.

The winner is whoever reaches the finishing line with their chicken still on their spoon.

* If you don't know any real chickens that want to play, use robot chickens.

SUBO WRESTLING

PLAYERS: 2

EQUIPMENT:

2 inflatable sumo suits

2 SuBo suits (i.e. outfits that Susan Boyle would wear around town)

MP3 of 'I Dreamed a Dream' on loop

INSTRUCTIONS:

Players put on the sumo suits, then the SuBo suits over the top.

Players stand within the sumo ring (called a dohyō, fact fans), and at the whistle, they wrestle.

The first player to step out of the ring or fall over is the loser.

Repeat until one player concedes because they can't stand to listen to 'I Dreamed a Dream' ever again.

PULL ME ALONG JUMP

★★★★★★★★

INSTRUCTIONS:

Line up players in pairs along the start line. The finish line is the length of a long jump away. One of players in each pair lies on the floor and holds onto the other player's leg.

When the whistle blows, the standing players have to move forward as fast as possible, dragging the other players along the floor.

The first pair to cross the finish line wins.

To ramp up the competition, play this game on a variety of different floors: in ascending order of difficulty try lino, carpet, grass, gravel.

BACK TO BACK RACING

INSTRUCTIONS:

The umpire ties pairs of players back to back. Whoever gets paired up with Linford Christie should be pretty happy about it.

When the starter pistol goes, the pairs of players have to race to the end of the racetrack.

The winner is probably going to be Linford Christie.

PLAYERS: Should be divided into pairs

EQUIPMENT:

Ropes, ties or belts to tie players together

Linford Christie

ELASTIC PING STING ✸✸✸✸✸✸

INSTRUCTIONS:

Each player strips to their pants. Then with the marker pen or lipstick they draw targets on their nipples and crotches.

Players stand facing each other two metres apart and take it in turns to fire elastic bands at the targets.

Score 20 for a hit on the nips, 50 for the crotch.

The winner is whoever scores the most points. Their prize is the salve to soothe their sore nips.

PAIN: 4

EQUIPMENT:

Elastic bands of various sizes and thickness

Marker pen or lipstick

Salve

PLAYERS: At least 2, but not so many that all the water spills out of the pool. Plus 1 lifeguard, because safety is paramount

TIME ALLOTTED: An allotted time

EQUIPMENT:

Lots of earmuffs

Swimming pool

MUFF DIVING

INSTRUCTIONS:

Scatter the earmuffs around the bottom of the pool/paddling pool/bathtub/puddle.

When the lifeguard blows the whistle, players have to dive (carefully) into the pool/paddling pool/bathtub/puddle and retrieve as many earmuffs as they can.

The player who has collected the most earmuffs at the end of the allotted time is the winner.

Players who wear earmuffs to play cannot count those earmuffs towards their earmuff total.

* If you can't get a swimming pool, use a paddling pool. If you can't get a paddling pool, use the bathtub. If you can't get a bathtub, use a puddle.

WARNING!
If you can't swim, get someone else to play this game for you

119

CAN YOU FEEL IT? ✹✹

Yes you can!

PLAYERS:

2 teams of 2

EQUIPMENT:

2 pairs of very tight lycra leggings

Mystery objects

INSTRUCTIONS:

Each team selects a person to be the Stuffer; the other is the Groper.

The Stuffer puts on a pair of leggings, selects one of the mystery objects and shoves it into the crotchular region of the leggings.

By feeling the Stuffer's crotch, the Groper wins a point for the team when they manage to guess the mystery object.

SAMPLE MYSTERY OBJECTS:

Stepladder
The Shard
Boa constrictor
Michelangelo's David
12" meatball sub

Bagpipes
Football World Cup
Tube of Pringles
Dildo

STEVE MCDONALD HAD A FARM ✳

PLAYERS: 2

EQUIPMENT:

Steve McDonald from *Coronation Street* or his identical twin Simon Gregson

The names of some animals, or the telephone number of Bill Oddie to ask him the names of some animals

Jack P. Shepherd from *Coronation Street*

TIME ALLOTTED: 20 seconds–50 years

INSTRUCTIONS:

You and Steve McDonald take it in turns to sing, 'Steve McDonald had a farm, E.I.E.I.O! And on that farm he had some (insert impression of animal).' The player wins a point if Jack P. Shepherd guesses which animal it is.

SAMPLE ANIMALS:

Camel   Otter
Fruit bat   Panda
Platypus   Dingo
Shark (technically a fish)
Snake

Incidentally, Steve does not own or even rent a farm. Jack however is a fully qualified Shepherd, with his own flock of prize-winning peas.

In the unlikely event that Steve and Jack are busy, two of you must change your names by deed poll to Steve McDonald and Jack P. Shepherd.

Christmas is the best time of the whole year, especially when you're a Celebrity Juice producer because you get to make the Celebrity Juice Christmas episodes, which are the best thing about the best time of the year! Join us to celebrate...

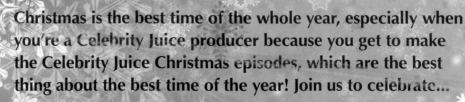

Christmas

Once you've had enough of rocking around the Christmas tree, gather around it instead, as there's festive fun for all the family when you play

★★

LICK MY BAUBLES

PLAYERS: All the family

DIFFICULTY: 2 (but 8 for Grandma, because she's old and her tastebuds don't work any more)

EQUIPMENT:

Christmas tree

Variety of substances (non-toxic)

INSTRUCTIONS:

Take the baubles off the Christmas tree.

Dip each bauble in one of the substances.

Each family member has to lick a bauble. They win a point if they can guess the mystery substance it was dipped in.

Repeat until the Queen's speech comes on the telly.

SUBSTANCES YOU COULD TRY:

Lemon juice
Tea
Vinegar
Cough mixture
Scrambled egg
Oil from a tin of sardines
Gravy

Christmas dinner can drag on longer than Alex Reid in the New Look sales. So keep your whole family amused by playing...

EAT, DRINK AND BE MESSY

★ ★ ★ ★ ★ ★ ★ ★ ★

DIFFICULTY: 7
(mainly because you're already feeling a bit sick and sleepy after stuffing yourself with Christmas food)

PLAYERS: Your family

EQUIPMENT:

Christmas dinner

Your mouth

INSTRUCTIONS:

Stuff your mouth full of Christmas dinner. DO NOT SWALLOW.

Sing a Christmas song (for example 'Deck the Halls with boughs of Holly Willoughbooby', 'Jingle Balls').

The first family member to guess the song you're singing through your gobful of food wins a point.

Repeat until you've run out of food, or until next Christmas.

123

Another fantastic episode of Celebrity Juice has just wrapped and now we want to celebrate. Join us! Strap on your dancing shoes, pick that spinach out of your teeth, and shake your ass down to Vodka Fog for the

DANCE Party

Don't name it on the sunshine,
Don't name it on the moonlight,
Don't name it on the good times...

NAME IT ON THE BOOGIE

★★★★★

PLAYERS: More than 2

EQUIPMENT:

Playlist of songs

Noise-cancelling headphones

INSTRUCTIONS:

Put on the noise-cancelling headphones.

Crank up the songs.

Through the medium of interpretive dance, the other players try to convey to you which song is playing.

If you correctly guess the name of the song, you win a point.

GET YOUR COAT, YOU'VE PULLED

That bottle of hot sauce has been making eyes at you all night across the dancefloor. It's nearly chucking-out time and you need to seal the deal.

INSTRUCTIONS:

You stand in the middle of the dancefloor.

One by one, the other players come up to you and try to seduce you in the style of a celebrity.

You win a point if you can guess which celebrity they are trying to be.

You both win if you cop off.

DIFFICULTY: Really depends on how trollied you are

PLAYERS: A club-full

EQUIPMENT: All in good working order

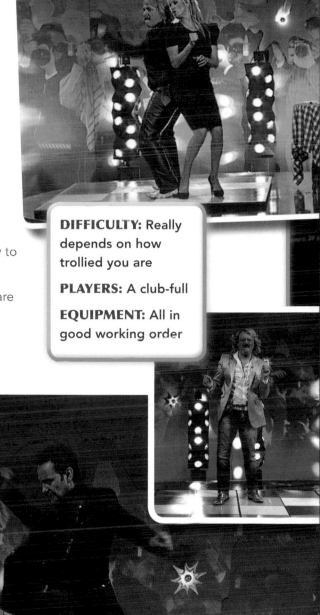

125

NUDGE THE JUDGE ★★★

PLAYERS: 2 teams of 4

EQUIPMENT: *The X Factor* judges' desk. If you can't get hold of one because *The X Factor* still needs it, cover your dining table with a sheet that reaches the floor and use that

INSTRUCTIONS:

One team sits behind the desk. They are the judges. Bagsy not to be Louis!

The other team chooses one member to be the nudger then sits down to watch.

The nudger hides under the desk and repeatedly nudges one of the judges, who has to try to maintain a poker face during the interference.

If the nudger's team can guess which judge is being nudged, they win a point. If they can't, the judges win a point.

Repeat until Joe McElderry gets the recognition he deserves.

TOUCH THE CARDBOARD GAME ★★

PLAYERS: 2 teams, plus 1 cardboard holder

EQUIPMENT: Piece of cardboard (any size)

INSTRUCTIONS:

One person is in charge of the cardboard.

At any given time, this person can hold out or throw the piece of cardboard and say: 'Touch the cardboard'.

The first player to touch the cardboard wins a point for their team.

Repeat til death or until the cardboard is destroyed.

WHAT'S IN FEARNE'S BRA?

Follow the string to find out what Cotton's stuffed into her bra to boost her boobs.

ANSWERS on the answers page p156

JED or alive?

Are the following famous people Jed (DEAD) or Alive (ALIVE)?

BARRY CHUCKLE
One half of comedy duo, the Chuckle Brothers. The short one.
Jed ☐ Alive ☐

DUSTIN 'SCREECH' DIAMOND
Star of *Saved By the Bell* and home porno *Saved By the Smell*
Jed ☐ Alive ☐

WONKEY DONKEY
from *SMTV Live*
Jed ☐ Alive ☐

WHIGFIELD
Danish one-hit wonder
Jed ☐ Alive ☐

KEN DODD
Toothy entertainer
Jed ☐ Alive ☐

SISQO
Thong fan
Jed ☐ Alive ☐

CHRISTOPHER LLOYD
from *Back to the Future*
Jed ☐ Alive ☐

QUEEN VICTORIA
star of the 19th century
Jed ☐ Alive ☐

JOHN LENNON
out of the Beatles
Jed ☐ Alive ☐

DISCLAIMER: The following people were alive or dead at the time of publication. We claim no responsibility for anyone that subsequently dies, or comes back from the dead.

ANSWERS on the answers page p159

AND THE SCORES AT THE END OF THE GAMES ARE...

Sha-ting

REWARD THE WINNER WITH THIS

write your scores here,
you dingbat

WHAT'S IN A NAME?

A lot of people ask us, 'How did you come up with the name 'Celebrity Juice'?'

Remember the theory that if you shut an infinite number of monkeys in a room with an infinite number of typewriters, they will eventually write the entire works of Shakespeare? Well, if you shut one monkey in a cupboard for an hour with a laptop and a variety pack of WKD, it comes up with the name *Celebrity Panel Show Starring Some Celebrities*. So we sent the monkey back into the cupboard and it thought up *Celebrity Juice* instead. Here are the original titles of some more of your favourite TV shows:

THE CUBE
The Cuboid

GREAT BRITISH BAKE-OFF
Yeast Inspection

HOW TO LOOK GOOD NAKED
Menopausal And Fabulous!

I'M A CELEBRITY...GET ME OUT OF HERE!
I Used To Be A Celebrity... Feed Me A Kangaroo's Bumhole!

DOCTOR WHO
Professor What

Reverend When

Archduke Where

Mc Why (Feat. DJ How)

MASTERCHEF: THE PROFESSIONALS
Michelin Man & Michelin-Starred Man

UNIVERSITY CHALLENGE
Virgins' Night Out

EMBARRASSING BODIES
Flapping Fannies, Warty Willies And Stinky Scrotcs

THE ANTIQUES ROADSHOW
Money For Old Rope

WHO WANTS TO BE A MILLIONAIRE?
Britain's Got Tarrant

COACH TRIP
Xenophobes On Tour

THE X FACTOR
Pop Idol

131

USES FOR
FEARNE'S NOSTRILS

It is a common misconception that Fearne Cotton has huge nostrils. This is not true. She has gigantic, award-winning mega nostrils. Her nostrils only look vaguely normal thanks to CGI and clever lighting. However, her gargantuan nose holes can be very useful as the following:

Nesting site for flamingos

North Korea's secret missile base

Cave for hibernating bears

Carpet World storage depot

Proposed extension for the Victoria line

Europe's largest bat sanctuary

Upside down umbrella stand

Upside down wishing well

Dump for depleted uranium rods

Spare Large Hadron Collider

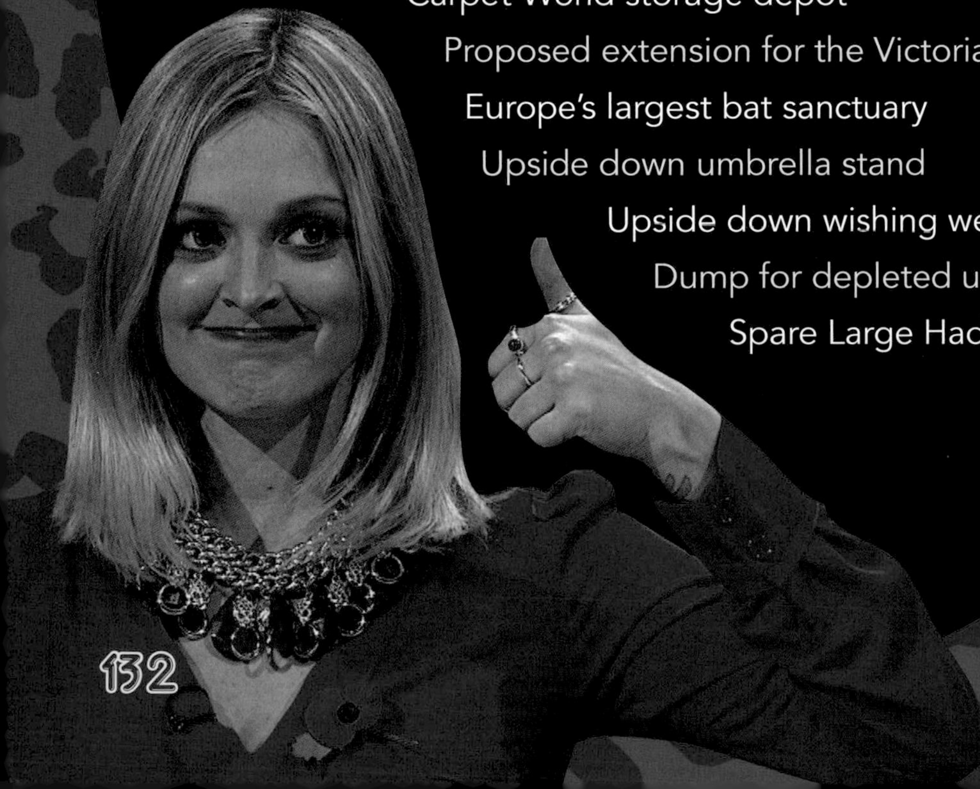

ASK THE PRODUCERS OF

The Producers of Celebrity Juice

Can I get a job on Celebrity Juice?
Dunno. Maybe. What sort of job?

Keith's moustache stylist?
Join the queue.

Where's the queue?
It starts over there, and finishes 400 miles away.

Are Holly's bangers real?
We definitely didn't imagine them.

So how is it possible that anything so magnificent exists?
We think that too every time we stare at them.

Where does Spud the Dog live when he's not on the show?
On a massive yacht moored off the coast of St Lucia.

Why does Keith often suggest watching parts of the show with a box of tissues? I've never cried once during Celebrity Juice.
Errrr...ask your mum when you're a bit older.

133

THE  GUIDE TO MAKING YOURSELF INTO A

★ **Spray Silly String into your hair, for the luxurious look of a headful of hair extensions on a budget.**

★ Stick Quality Street wrappers all over your body for an inexpensive vajazzle.

★ **Hold a flashing bike lamp by your face, to emulate the paps papping you constantly.**

★ When people try talk to you, shout 'No pictures!' then hide behind a massive pair of shades.

★ **Get your own entourage. It's fine to start out small – your nan and a** handful of her friends from Bridge Club will suffice.

★ Alternatively, get the look of an entourage following you around by attaching £5 notes to the hem of your coat with fishing wire and trailing them along the ground behind you.

★ **If it's not a fad diet, don't eat it.**

★ Wear the most impractical high-heeled shoes you can find. Walking is for Normals.

★ **Better still, pay a couple of people to carry you everywhere in a sedan chair.**

134

- Keep a roll of red carpet up your trouser leg, then unfurl it wherever you go to turn even the dowdiest occasion into a glamorous event.

- **When trying to crash a VIP party, tell the security guard you're one of the Kardashian sisters or Baldwin brothers. Nobody can keep track of them all.**

- Failing that, pretend you're Samuel L. Jackson. Who wouldn't let Shaft into a party?

- **If they don't fall for that either, hold important shouty fake phonecalls with your agent. Try saying, 'Tell them I'm not doing it for less than half a mil and points. Sorry, can you hold, my stylist is trying to get through.'**
TIP: Avoid trying this in places where there is no reception, like the London underground. Also remember to switch your phone to flight mode so it doesn't ring when you're doing this, otherwise people will realise you're a dingbat.

- **Use the expression 'Do you know who I am?' as often as you can. NB: you must make sure to be well dressed when saying it and you must not sound confused. And never try this when visiting an old people's home.**

- Be born and raised in a place, and hope that in twenty years a television company will make a reality TV series in that place.

- **Befriend somebody who is only a celebrity because they starred in a sex tape, then leak your own sex tape.**

135

TOP 10 MOST SHOCKING MOMENTS OF

10. KEITH'S DATE WITH PAMELA ANDERSON

It finally happened: Pamela Anderson from *Baywatch* and home movies finally agreed to go on a date with Keith, albeit in front of a live studio audience. They bonded over a mutual love of cows, turnips and grass. We don't know whether it went much further, because a gentleman doesn't mott and tell.

9. VERNON KAY PLAYING WHAT'S VERN ON?

Could Mr Saturday Night, Vernon Kay, work out what he was sitting on through the power of bum touch alone?

8. JASON BIGGS FINGERING PIES

Jason Biggs from the *American Pie* films fingered various pies and had to guess what was inside. But he didn't stop there, oh no, he stared straight at Fearne and fingered that pie like nobody's business. Poor old Fearne! Or, depending upon your personal taste, lucky old Fearne.

7. FEARNE GETTING HER TOES SUCKED

This one was a particular favourite with the boys! Fearne guessed that her toes had been shoved inside a chicken... but no, it was just Keith giving them a little suck.

6. LUNATIC SUPERFANS WITH JLS

We persuaded two JLS superfans to put on straitjackets and face masks, then we wheeled them onto the stage on a trolley like the dangers to society that they clearly are. All this for the chance to win tickets to a JLS gig. Have they never heard of Ticketmaster?

TOP 10

5. STEPHEN MULHERN AND KONNIE HUQ INTERVIEWING KEITH IN HIS DRESSING ROOM

We asked Steve and Konnie to interview Keith in his dressing room before the show. And failed to tell them he'd be naked. Not sure how that slipped our mind.

4. KEITH KISSES YVETTE FIELDING

Keith somehow managed to convince celebrity ghost botherer Yvette Fielding to give him a snog. The scariest thing filmed in night vision since *Blair Witch Project*.

3. HOLLY AND KELLY BROOK PLAY KEITH'S COCKTAIL

Holly and Kelly Brook compete to find a drinking straw using just their mouth whilst blindfolded. Except Keith switched the straw with a giant dildo. Clever.

2. WHAT'S UNDER KEITH'S NIGHTIE?

True fact: We didn't know exactly what Keith had under his nightie that caused the panellists such shock when he flashed them. Then he showed us all and we wished we still didn't know. We'll never eat Parma ham again.

1. ANT AND DEC IN A BOX WITH A NAKED CHEF

Who can forget the face Dec pulled when he yanked off his blindfold and realised that he had been feeling up a naked old woman? If you have succeeded in forgetting, then refresh your memory by looking at the picture.

Like Christopher Columbus, Magellan, Marco Polo and Uncle Travelling Matt from *Fraggle Rock*, Celebrity Juice has swept the globe. It is the number one show in every single country* BAR NONE.** Take a look at how our producer friends abroad make

AROUND THE WORLD

'You tosSOR....or if you're British: tosser.'

* Not yet true at time of publication.
** None is a small island off Norway with incredibly prudish inhabitants.

'Potato! Potato! Potato! Potato! Potato'
Translation: 'Hello and welcome to Irish Celebrity Juice! Potato!'

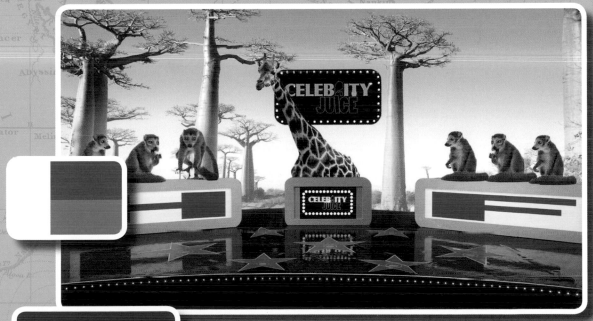

MADAGASCAR

'No I'm not Marvin from JLS, I'm an actual giraffe.'

CANADA

'Who are you calling a moose?'

EASTER ISLAND

'The first round is GiantStoneHead...
you will see a graphic of my giant stone
head divided into sectors...'

INDIA

'You're Bangratidy.'

ANTARCTICA

'And the scores at the end of that round are freez-ingggg!'

THE MOON

'Buzz Aldrin if you know the answer...'

BRAZIL

'For the 735th week running you have chosen
to play the topless beach volleyball round!'

ROMANIA

'You bunch of dingbats...I mean, bats.'

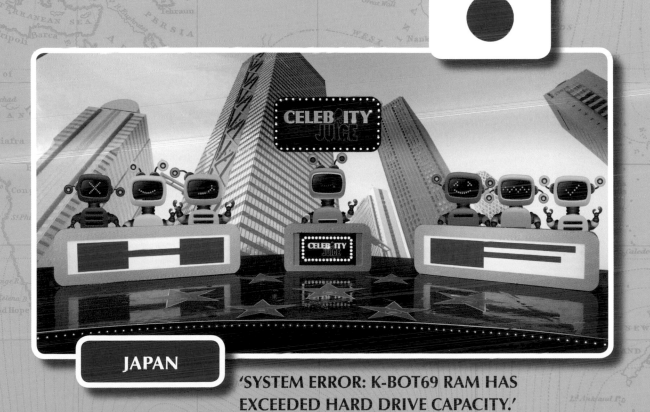

JAPAN

'SYSTEM ERROR: K-BOT69 RAM HAS
EXCEEDED HARD DRIVE CAPACITY.'

145

THE CELEBRITY JUICE
AUDIENCE

Like *The Cosby Show* and the FA Cup Final, Celebrity Juice is filmed in front of a live studio audience, and one day, YOU could be in it.

This is providing you apply for tickets, get tickets, don't lose the tickets down a sewer, don't get eaten by a bear on your way to the studio, don't fall into a dead faint just because you're in the same building as Fearne Cotton and Holly Willoughbooby, or get a better offer that evening.

But once you're inside the hallowed Celebrity Juice studio, how should you behave? We producers have watched well over a hundred Celebrity Juices being recorded, and have analysed the behaviour of well over a hundred audiences to tell you how you can be the perfect audience member.

DON'T

DO

DON'T	DO
✗ DON'T sit near Fearne's nostrils because you might get sucked in. They have their own weather system.	✔ DO sit near the front so you can get a good view of Holly's boobs, two of the seven wonders of the world.
✗ DON'T bring your mam if she will be offended by the language.	✔ DO bring your mam if she's bang tidy.
✗ DON'T be surprised when the show takes nine hours to record. It's still quicker than *8 Out of 10 Cats*.	✔ DO bring *Puzzler* magazine to keep yourself amused whilst the nine hour recording flies by.
✗ DON'T drink before the recording. You will not be allowed toilet privileges.	✔ DO wear an adult nappy if you think hanging on is going to be a problem.
✗ DON'T ask for Spud the Dog's autograph.	✔ DO ask someone for a cloth to clean Spud's mess off your shoe.
✗ DON'T stroke Keith's moustache.	✔ DO stroke Fearne's moustache.
✗ DON'T tell anyone what really goes on in that recording studio.	✔ DO tell everyone that it was even better than your wedding night.
✗ DON'T cry.	✔ DO laugh.

CELEBRITY JUICE   10 BUMMINGTON PLACE, MOTTSVILLE

FREQUENTLY ASKED
QUESTIONS
ABOUT

CELEBRITY JUICE

Can I come on Celebrity Juice?
Are you a celebrity?

Er...yes!
Really?

Sure!
Really?

...No.
Then no.

Does Celebrity Juice count towards your 5 a day?
No.

How do you pronounce 'Celebrity Juice'?
'Celebrity Juice'.

What flavour is Celebrity Juice?
A sharp topnote of citrus, with an undertone of ball sweat.

Can you send me some autographed photos of Holly naked?
No. Try eBay.

Is Fearne 100% cotton?
She certainly is. Her thread count is 1,500 and she is machine washable at 40 degrees.

Why do I get a burning sensation when I go to the loo?
You need to stop using your toilet seat as a barbecue.

Who would win in a fight between Holly and Fearne?
Well. Holly could overpower Fearne by smothering her with her sumptuous bangers. But Fearne could sniff Holly right up into her nostrils. We're calling it a draw.

Is Gino D'Acampo really from Huddersfield?
No, that was one of Keith's jokes.

So where is Gino actually from?
Sheffield.

I've heard that Spud is not really called Spud, apparently it's just his stage name. Is this true?
Yes. His real name is Liza Minnelli.

Is Danny Dyer's real name Malcolm Smith?
Yes. Go on, ask him yourself.

Why is Danny Dyer so angry?
Must've been something he ate.

Who books the guests?
Definitely not Keith, so stop asking him when One Direction are coming on because he's getting really pissed off.

When are One Direction coming on?
Piss off.

Everyone knows you're a massive fan of Celebrity Juice, which means that your mum, dad, sister, brother, nephew, first cousin, second cousin, aunty, uncle, godmother, grandfather, grandmother, step-grandmother, ex, social worker and boss all got you a copy of this book for your birthday.

This means you can keep one copy upstairs, one downstairs, one in the loo, one in the glove box of the car, one in the loo at work, one for Sunday best, and one spare – but what are you going to do with all the other copies? Happily, there are plenty of...

alternative USES for THE CELEBRITY JUICE BOOK

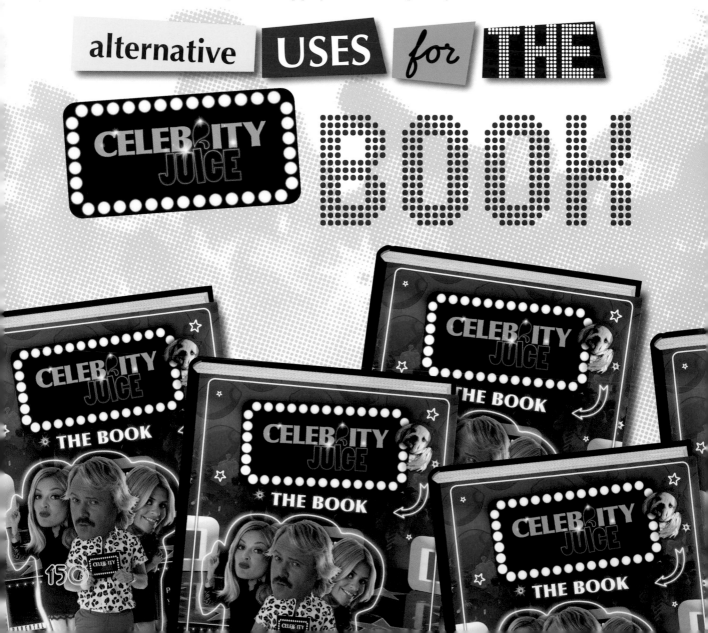

★ Save yourself some money: rearrange all the words into the same order as the latest bestseller and hey presto, you have a brand new book for free!

★ **Use it to create a papier mâché bust of your favourite Celebrity Juice star. Like a bust of Holly's bust.**

★ Take it onto *Antiques Roadshow* and try to pass it off as a first edition Bible.

★ **Cut out the words and glue them into ransom notes.**

★ Cut eye holes through it and peer over the garden fence to spy on your hot neighbour sunbathing.

★ **Sort out your wobbly table. If one of its legs is shorter than the others, simply use the sharp edges on the paper to cut down the other three.**

★ Make it into a really short skate ramp.

★ **Make it into a really short surfboard.**

★ If you've got enough spare copies, retile your roof with them.

★ **Enter it into *Britain's Got Talent* and watch it come third.**

Dicktionary

'Ginger!' Phrase most often used by Fearne, who has observed that there is a slight discrepancy in colour between the hair on Keith's head, which is blond, and his moustache, which appears to be tinged with gingerness.

Strawberry blond The correct term for any ginger hair that is growing on Keith.

Opening titles The bit after the man gives the nudity and offensive language warning, but before the bit where the show starts with Keith running down the stairs, pushing the @celebjuice logo away as he goes. The opening titles are there to give everyone enough time to shoo their granny out of the room, top up their drink, get a box of tissues if Kelly Brook is on, and settle into their seat braced for the show.

@celebjuice logo Thing for Keith to kick.

An allotted time Time allotted for panellists to play a game. The allotted time lasts for the length of time which has been allotted.

'Coming up after the break' The bit which shows you a good bit from the next part to stop you pissing off during the ad break because you can't stand to watch any more promos for dance music compilation albums or trails for *TOWIE*.

'I'm off for a shit, see you in a bit' Keith likes to have a poo or a wee during every ad break, and he also likes to tell it as it is. If he's going for a poo, he'll see you in two, but if he's going for a wee, he'll see you in three. That's not a mistake: Keith takes longer to wee than poo.

'Don't be a dingbat' A dingbat is a very stupid person. One should aim to never be a dingbat, unless playing the game 'Be a Dingbat', in which case one would be a dingbat to not be a dingbat because the aim is to be a dingbat. And if you don't follow that, you are the dingbat.

Sector (or, if you're American, secTOR) A sector (or, if you're American, secTOR) is a segment which is defined in size by its perimeter (or, if you're American, perimiTOR). Panellists pick a secTOR by pressing their buzzer (or, if you're American, buzzOR).

'I'll go get the prop, it's behind these curtains… these beef curtains" In the Lemon Head round, when a panellist chooses a sector (or, if you're American, SecTOR), it most often lands on 'Prop'. This is pure chance, and has nothing to do with the fact that visual props often make better telly than, say, the Headline sector.

The beef curtains which unveil the prop are made out of very thin strips of beef sewn together by Wandsworth Prison inmates. Only after using the beef curtains four times were we informed that 'beef curtains' are actually a euphemism for a lady's minge. Needless to say we all felt very embarrassed.

Sha-tingggg! Voice command. Triggers the machine which makes the scores drop from the top of the screen. The scores are added up by Carol Vorderman who actually still uses an abacus, which she calls Jane.

Panellist As soon as a celebrity's footsteps upon the hallowed Celebrity Juice stage, they waive all rights to be thought of as a celebrity or even in fact as a human being. They are now 'a panellist'. Thanks to a legal loophole, this gives us the right to play any game with them or for Keith to say anything about them without being sued.

Magazine guest A person who is either on their way up the road to Celebrity or, more commonly, on their way down the road from Celebrity. Ability to say the selected category out loud, without stumbling, is encouraged but not essential. We all remember the time when that dingbat NAME REDACTED BY LAWYERS turned up and he could barely stand up without holding onto the wall…although it was funny when he took a piss in the plant pot in Fearne's dressing room.

'They'll do it if they can go on the panel' The response from the agent of a celebrity who's been offered a spot as a magazine guest. NB: This negotiation technique has never actually worked.

Potato! Pronounced 'potato'. Exclamation normally used whilst in the presence of, or whilst talking about, a person of Irish persuasion. This is because when in Dublin, it is impossible to eat anywhere without being served potatoes. Potato!

'Choose a categORy' Each week Keith invites the panellists to choose a categORy from the giant magazine. The panellists always choose a categORy from the top of the magazine, but this is NOT because there are no holes cut in the bottom of the magazine. It would be too low for anyone other than Verne Troyer to get their head out of without lying on the floor.

'Buzz in if you know the answer. If you don't know the answer, be a chancer and buzz in anyway' The instruction at the start of the buzzer round to encourage the less intelligent* panellists to have a go at answering the questions.** Otherwise they won't say a word in part three of the show so we have to use lots of shots of them gormlessly laughing at everyone else.

Incredible Hulk's anus For our game In Your Face we use the actual costume used in the *Incredible Hulk* film. The anus section of the costume is the perfect size for our purposes. As you can see, Katie Price has her entire face pushed through the arsehole of a very large man (not for the first time) and she is loving it.

---

* Again, it would be rude to name names here; all we'll say is that one J. Swash could have listened a bit more in school.

** The answer 'Harry Styles' will 50% of the time win a point for the team, so the panellist may as well give that a go.

Jackson Five Bush An (ex) Celebrity Juice production team member recalls with horror the time they walked in on Holly getting changed and thought she had a member of the Jackson Five stood in front of her. It was, however, just her bush. The (ex) production team member has spent the last two years on sick leave and is costing the production a fortune in psychiatric bills.

'What's the message?' Exploratory query to probe beneath the surface of a guest when they are shamelessly plugging their CD/DVD/TV show/film/book/download/clothing range/perfume/kitchenware/lifestyle website etc. Keith asks this question because he wants to know the motivation and truth behind every artistic endeavour by his guests, and is desperate to delve deep inside their psyches.

'What are the peripherals?' Guests often confuse the peripherals with 'the message' and start talking about the peripherals of the message of their product when, of course, the message and peripherals are completely different, as we're sure you know.

'See you down the Hippodrome, Gary/Spud' Keith's sign-off to his dog Gary (R.I.P), later Spud. The Hippodrome is where Keith likes to take his dog for a few jars after work. And if you're worried about an underaged dog drinking in a pub, don't be - he's got a very convincing fake ID.

'Back to me in the studio' This originated when we thought we had cracked time travel. Keith planned to travel back in time each week to take on Jedward in a challenge and then travel straight back to the present day to make the teams guess who won the challenge.

Disappointingly, what we thought was a hole in the space time continuum turned out to be simply a rip in the crotch of Keith's trousers.

'I would smash your back doors in' When a man and lady love each other very very much, they may decide to take their lovemaking to the next level. To tell someone that you would 'smash their back doors in' means that you could imagine being so in love with that person, so consumed with passion and respect for that person, that you'd want to make your love even stronger...

Oooosh Pronounced "Oooosh".

ANSWERS

Well, how did you do? Check your answers here:

CELEBRITY PIZZA FACE

1 Lady Gaga

2 Craig David

3 Susan Boyle

4 Ke$ha

5 Holly Willoughbooby

SUBOKU

DIRTY WORDSEARCH

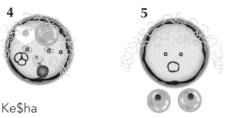

Backdoors	Bush	Nipple
Ballbag	Clitoris	Rimjob
Bangers	Flaps	Tallywhacker
Bellend	Minge	Teabag
Boobs	Mott	Titwank

HOW WELL DO YOU KNOW CELEBRITY JUICE? QUIZ

1. A	2. D
3. C	4. A
5. D	6. C
7. B	8. C
9. C	10. B
11. C	12. D
13. A	14. C

DOGGY STYLE

1. Dot Cotton
2. The Queen
3. Hulk Hogan
4. Ozzy Osbourne
5. Mr T
6. Nicki Minaj
7. Pat Butcher
8. Russell Brand
9. Jedward

SPOT THE DIFFERENCE

They're both the same, you dingbat!

WHO ARE YOU KIDDING?

1. Kelly Brook
2. Beyoncé
3. Amanda Holden
4. Chris Evans
5. Aston Merrygold
6. Matt Cardle
7. Malcolm Smith
8. Russell Crowe
9. Mr T
10. Daniel Craig
11. Keanu Reeves
12. Jedward
13. Charlie Sheen
14. Angelina Jolie
15. Niall Horan
16. Prince Harry

IS VERNE BIGGER THAN?

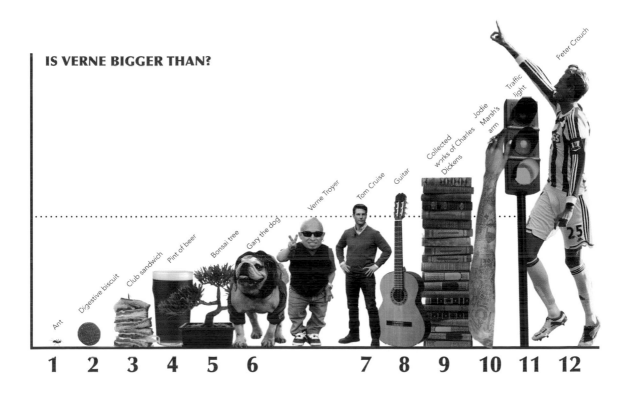

1   2   3   4   5   6   7   8   9   10   11   12

157

HOW WELL DO YOU KNOW CELEBRITY JUICE? QUIZ

1. B
2. B
3. A
4. B
5. D
6. D
7. B (Bonus point answer: A)
8. A
9. C
10. C
11. A
12. A

COCKWORD

STICKY BITS

DOT-TO-DOT

158

WHAT'S MY NAHHHME?

Russell Brand   Lady Gaga   Tom Cruise

WHO'S BEEN RAMMED?

Justin Bieber   Jeremy   Angelina
                 Clarkson   Jolie

WHAT'S IN MY MCFLY?

Trumpet, Badger, Scandinavia, Baguette/
Garlic

SPOT THE GOLDEN POTATO

Did you find the Golden Potato?
No? Then go back and read the
book again, you dingbat!

JOEY ESSEX: THE QUIZ

1. A
2. B
3. A
4. C
5. C
6. B
7. A
8. B
9. B
10. B

WHAT'S IN FEARNE'S BRA?

JED OR ALIVE?

BARRY CHUCKLE: Alive. Otherwise the
surviving Chuckle would have to perform
as the Chuckle Brother.
SCREECH: Alive, though not been seen
for a while.
WONKEY DONKEY: Alive but in rehab.
WHIGFIELD: Alive.
KEN DODD: Alive.
SISQO: Alive.
CHRISTOPHER LLOYD: Alive, but NB: he
could have died and then come back from
the future so that he was alive again.
QUEEN VICTORIA: Dead.
JOHN LENNON: Dead.